by US Army

by US Armed Forces

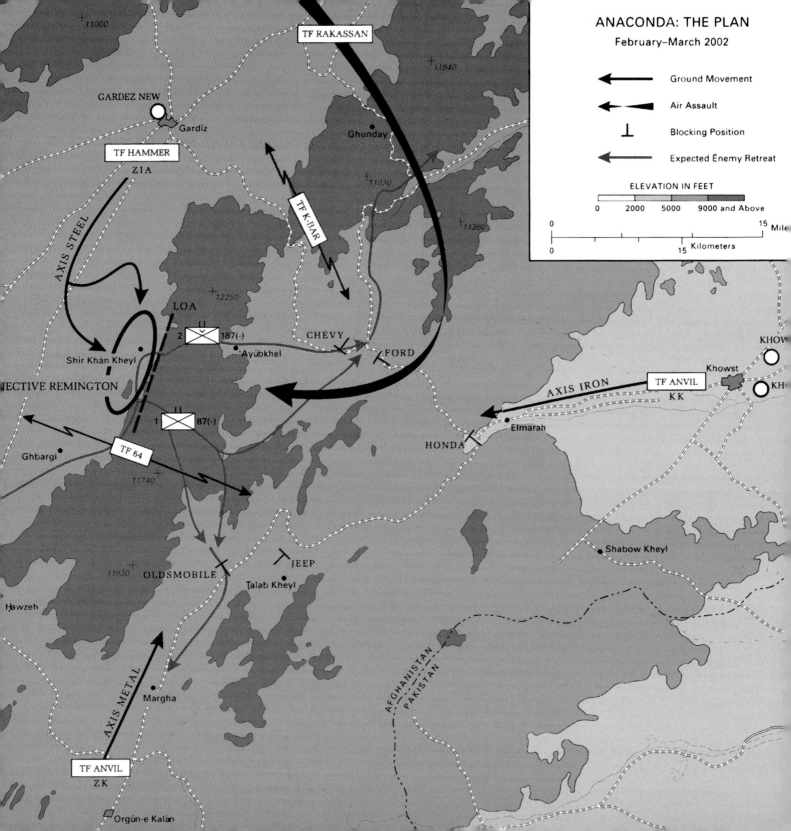

ANACONDA: THE PLAN
February–March 2002

by US Navy

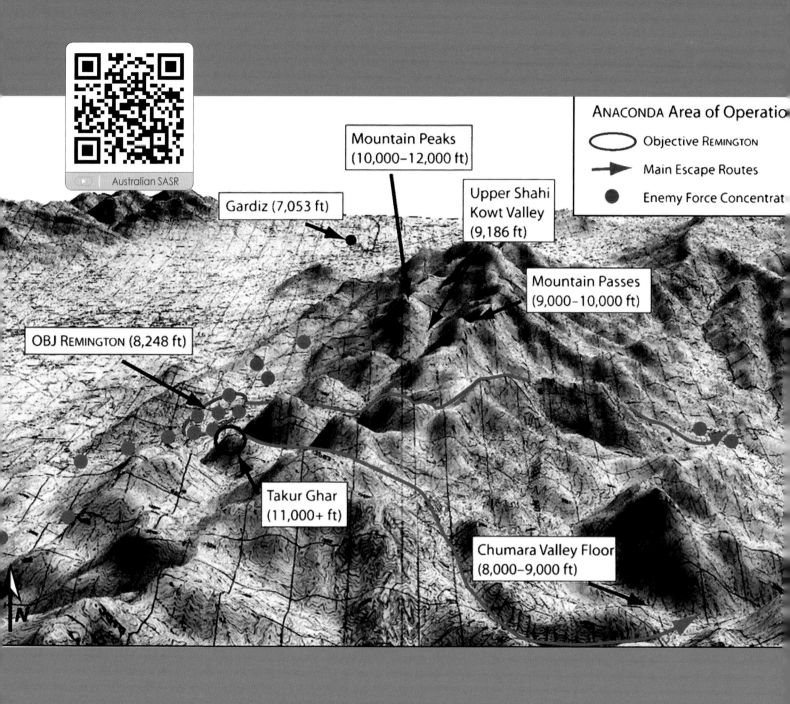

Australian SASR

ANACONDA Area of Operatio

⬭ Objective REMINGTON

→ Main Escape Routes

● Enemy Force Concentrat

Mountain Peaks
(10,000–12,000 ft)

Gardiz (7,053 ft)

Upper Shahi
Kowt Valley
(9,186 ft)

Mountain Passes
(9,000–10,000 ft)

OBJ REMINGTON (8,248 ft)

Takur Ghar
(11,000+ ft)

Chumara Valley Floor
(8,000–9,000 ft)

N

by US Armed Forces

Anaconda

Apres les attentats du 11 septembre à New York, la première réaction des États-Unis fut de vouloir capturer en Afghanistan Oussama Ben Laden, leader d'Al Qaeda, l'organisation islamiste djihadiste qui a organisé le massacre. Face à la position du gouvernement taliban, refusant de leur livrer Ben Laden, les États-Unis ont commencé la première phase de la Guerre contre le Terrorisme, appelée également Opération Liberté Durable, avec le soutien de l'OTAN et des Nations Unies. Le 13 novembre 2001, deux mois seulement après les attentats, Kaboul, capitale afghane, était prise par les forces de la coalition internationale, mais Ben Laden demeurait introuvable.

Les forces d'occupation ont commencé alors une série d'attaques sélectives sur des zones où les forces d'Al Qaeda étaient cachées à l'est de l'Afghanistan, un territoire agreste et montagneux jouxtant le Pakistan. Entre le 1er et le 18 mars 2002 a lieu l'Opération Anaconda, où les forces de la « 101 Airbone Division », de la « 10th Mountain Division », canadienne et d'opérations spéciales de plusieurs pays alliés ont occupé la vallée de Shahi-Kot dans la bataille de Takur Ghar. Même si les disparitions ennemies ont été considérables et toutes ses défenses ont été détruites, Oussama Ben Laden n'a pas été capturé. La guerre continue.

Dopo gli attentati dell'11 settembre a New York, la prima reazione degli USA fu quella di catturare in Afganistan Osama Bin Laden, il leader di Al Qaeda, l'organizzazione islamista jihadista che organizzò il massacro. Come reazione al rifiuto di consegnare Bin Laden da parte del governo talebano, gli USA iniziarono la prima fase della Guerra contro il Terrorismo, chiamata anche Operazione Libertà Duratura, con l'appoggio della NATO e delle Nazioni Unite. Il 13 novembre del 2001, soltanto due mesi dopo gli attentati, Kabul, la capitale afgana, era conquistata dalle forze della coalizione internazionale, ma Bin Laden rimaneva latitante.

Le forze d'occupazione iniziarono allora una serie di attacchi selettivi contro delle zone in cui si nascondevano i guerriglieri di Al Qaeda nell'est dell'Afganistan, un territorio agricolo e montagnoso al confine con il Pakistan. Tra il 1 e il 18 marzo del 2002 ebbe luogo l'Operazione Anaconda, nella quale le forze della "101 Airborne Division", della "10th Mountain Division" canadese e quelle addette alle operazioni speciali di vari paesi alleati occuparono la valle di Shahi-Kot, nella battaglia di Takur Ghar. Nonostante le vittime nemiche siano state considerevoli e tutte le difese distrutte, Osama Bin Laden non fu catturato. La guerra è ancora in corso.

ニューヨークの9月11日の多発同時テロ事件の後、報復のためにアメリカが最初に行ったことのひとつが、首謀者であるアル・カーイダのリーダーであるビン・ラディンを、潜伏していると思われるアフガニスタンで捕らえることでした。しかし、タリバン政権がその引渡しを拒否したため、アメリカは、これらのテロに対抗するための戦争を始めました。この戦争は、北大西洋条約機構や国連によっても支持されたものでした。2001年11月13日、ニューヨークのテロからわずか2ヵ月後、アフガニスタンの首都カブールは多国籍軍によって占領されましたが、ビン・ラディンは、相変わらず見つかりませんでした。

そこで、多国籍軍は、アル・カーイダが潜んでいると思われた、パキスタンとの国境近くの険しい山岳地帯であるアフガニスタンの東部を中心に攻撃を開始することにしました。2002年3月1日から18日、「アナコンガ作戦」が開始され、アメリカ軍の第101空挺師団やカナダ人部隊などから構成された多国籍軍の特別部隊は、タクール・ガールでの戦いに突入しました。しかし、イラク軍の犠牲者は多数を数え、その軍事基地を破壊したものの、オサマ・ビン・ラディンは見つかりませんでした。そして今日でも、このアメリカを中心としたタリバンに対する反テロ戦争は続いています。

fra ⓘ Article Wikipèdia

ita ⓘ Articolo Wikipedia

jap ⓘ ウィキペディアの記事

Timeline Video

by US Navy

2002 Operation Anaconda
Central Asia – War of Afganistan

Tras los atentados del 11 de Septiembre en Nueva York la primera reacción de los EEUU fue la de capturar en Afganistán a Osama Bin Laden, líder de Al Qaeda, la organización islamista yihadista que organizó la masacre. Ante la negativa de entregar a Bin Laden por parte del gobierno Talibán, los EEUU inician la primera fase de la Guerra contra el Terrorismo, también denominada Operación Libertad Duradera, con el apoyo de la OTAN y Naciones Unidas. El 13 de noviembre de 2001, tan sólo dos meses después de los atentados, Kabul, la capital afgana, era tomada por las fuerzas de la coalición internacional, pero Bin Laden continuaba en paradero desconocido.

Las fuerzas de ocupación iniciaron entonces una serie de ataques selectivos a zonas donde las fuerzas de Al Qaeda permanecían escondidas al este de Afganistán, un territorio agreste y montañoso que linda con Pakistán. Entre el 1 y el 18 de marzo de 2002 tiene lugar la Operación Anaconda, en la que fuerzas de la "101 Airborne Division", de la "10th Mountain Division", canadienses y de operaciones especiales de varios países aliados ocuparon el valle de Shahi-Kot en la batalla de Takur Ghar. Aunque las bajas enemigas fueron considerables y se destruyeron todas sus defensas Osama Bin Laden no fue capturado. La guerra todavía continúa.

After September 11 attacks in New York, the United States' first reaction was to capture Osama Bin Laden - Al Qaeda leader - in Afghanistan. Al Qaeda had been the Islamic Yihadist organization which organized the massacre. As the Taliban rulers refuse to hand over Bin Laden, the United States starts the first phase of the War against Terrorism, the also called "Operation Enduring Freedom", supported by the NATO and the UN. On November 13, 2001, only two months after the attacks, Kabul, the Afghan capital, was taken by the international coalition forces, but nobody knew where Bin Laden was.

Occupation forces started then a series of selective attack to areas where the Al Qaeda forces remained hidden, East of Afghanistan, a wild and hilly land which borders on Pakistan. Between March 1 and 18, 2002, the Anaconda Operation takes place. There, the "101 Airborne Division" forces, belonging to the "10th Mountain Division", from Canada and several allied countries, occupied the Shahi-Kot Valley in the battle of Takur Ghar. Although the enemy casualties were considerable and all their defences were destroyed, Osama Bin Laden was not captured. The war is still in progress.

Nach den Attentaten vom 11. September in New York war die erste Reaktion der USA die Gefangennahme von Osama Bin Laden in Afghanistan, dem Anführer der Al Quaeda, der islamistischen Yihad-Organisation, die für das Massaker verantwortlich war. Die Taliban-Regierung weigerte sich, Bin Laden auszuliefern, woraufhin die USA die erste Kriegsphase gegen den Terrorismus einläutete, die auch die Operation Dauerhafter Frieden genannt wurde und die Unterstützung der NATO und der Vereinten Nationen hatte. Am 13. November 2001, nur zwei Monate nach den Attentaten, wurde die afghanische Hauptstadt Kabul von den Truppen der internationalen Koalition eingenommen, aber Bin Laden befand sich weiterhin an einem unbekannten Aufenthaltsort.

Darauf hin begannen die Besatzer eine Reihe selektiver Angriffe auf Gebiete, in denen sich die Kräfte der Al Qaeda im Osten Afghanistans versteckt hielten, ein unwirtliches, bergiges Gelände, das an Pakistan angrenzt. Zwischen dem 1. und 18. März 2002 findet die Operation Anaconda statt, während der die Kräfte der „101 Airborne Division", der „10th Mountain Division" aus Kanada und der Spezialoperationen verschiedener alliierter Länder das Tal von Shahi-Kot während der Schlacht von Takur Ghar einnahmen. Obwohl es bei den Feinden viele Tote gab und die gesamte feindliche Abwehr zerstört wurde, wurde Osama bin Laden nicht gefangen genommen. Der Krieg ist noch nicht zu Ende.

esp · Artículo Wikipedia

eng · Wikipedia Article

deu · Wikipedia-Artikel

OPERATION ANACONDA

2002

Powell, Schwarzkopf and Wolfowitz at Cheney press conference, February 1991
by US Armed Forces

Military personnel examine the tail section of a scud missile shot down by an MIM-104 Patriot Air Defense missile during Operation Desert Storm (ODS). (Photo by Combat Camera)

by US Armed Forces

Gulf War

by US Armed Forces

by US Armed Forces

© Christiaan Briggs

by US Armed Forces

by US Armed Forces

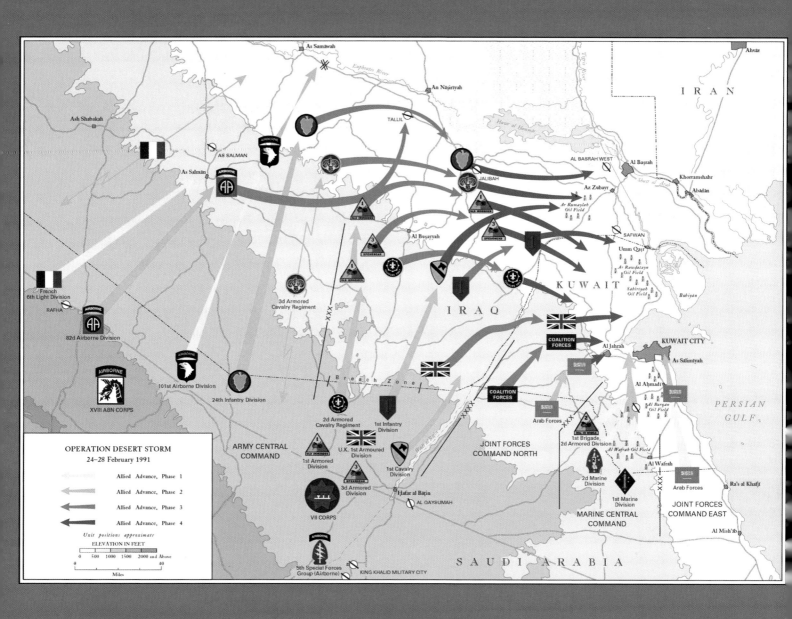

OPERATION DESERT STORM
24–28 February 1991

Allied Advance, Phase 1
Allied Advance, Phase 2
Allied Advance, Phase 3
Allied Advance, Phase 4

Unit positions approximate

ELEVATION IN FEET

0   500 1000 1500 2000 and Above

0   40

Miles

IRAN

As Samāwah
Euphrates River
An Nāṣirīyah
Hawr al Ḥammār
Tigris River
Ahvāz
TALLIL
AL BASRAH WEST
Al Basrah
Khorramshahr
Ābādān
Shatt al Arab
JALIBAH
Az Zubayr
Ar Rumaylah Oil Field
SAFWAN
Umm Qaṣr
Ar Rawdatayn Oil Field
Ṣabiriyah Oil Field
Būbiyān
KUWAIT
PERSIAN GULF
KUWAIT CITY
As Salimīyah
Al Ahmadī
Al Burqan Oil Field
Al Wafrah Oil Field
Al Wafrah
Ra's al Khafjī
Al Mish'āb

Ash Shabakah
AS SALMAN
As Salmān
Al Buṣayyah
Al Jahrah
COALITION FORCES
COALITION FORCES
JOINT FORCES COMMAND NORTH
Arab Forces
1st Brigade, 2d Armored Division
2d Marine Division
1st Marine Division
MARINE CENTRAL COMMAND
Arab Forces
JOINT FORCES COMMAND EAST

French 6th Light Division
RAFHA
82d Airborne Division
101st Airborne Division
24th Infantry Division
XVIII ABN CORPS

3d Armored Cavalry Regiment
Breach Zone

IRAQ

ARMY CENTRAL COMMAND

2d Armored Cavalry Regiment
1st Infantry Division
1st Armored Division
3d Armored Division
VII CORPS

1st Cavalry Division

U.K. 1st Armoured Division

Wall of Berm

Ḥafar al Bāṭin
Al Qaysūmah

5th Special Forces Group (Airborne)
KING KHALID MILITARY CITY

SAUDI ARABIA

by US Armed Forces

NOMENCLATURE
T-72 MAIN BATTLE TANK
MAIN GUN: 125MM GUN
BASIC LOAD: 44 RDS
WEIGHT: 41000 KG
CREW: 3

⊙

En général, l'appellation « Tempête du désert » fait référence aux opérations terrestres menées entre le 24 et le 28 février 1991 par la coalition internationale pour rendre la souveraineté au Koweït envahi par l'Irak une année auparavant. La coalition, composée par 31 pays et menée par les États-Unis sous le mandat de l'ONU, a commencé les attaques avec une longue série de bombardements sur des points stratégiques afin de débiliter la capacité offensive de l'ennemi.

La campagne terrestre proprement dite n'a commencé que lorsque le haut commandement de la coalition a déterminé que les conditions favorables étaient satisfaites. L'attaque fut un véritable étalage de stratégie conçu par le général américain Norman Schwarzkopf et son état-major. Après voir disposé face aux côtes de Koweït une importante force de Marines pour faire croire aux Iraquiens un débarquement imminent, les troupes de Saddam Hussein ont été flanquées par l'ouest, dans le propre désert iraquien, dans le but de couper ainsi les voies d'approvisionnement des troupes d'occupation au Koweït. L'attaque fut fulminante, en seulement 4 jours tout était fini. Plus de 100 000 soldats iraquiens se sont rendus en masse. Ils laissaient derrière eux des milliers de morts face à seulement quelques pertes de la coalition. Le concept de guerre avait changé.

⊙

In genere la denominazione "Tormenta del Deserto" si riferisce alle operazioni terrestri portate a termine tra il 24 e il 28 febbraio del 1991 dalla coalizione internazionale per restituire la sovranità al Kuwait, invaso dall'Iraq un anno prima. La coalizione, composta da 31 paesi e capeggiata dagli USA con il mandato dell'ONU, iniziò gli attacchi con una lunga serie di bombardamenti su dei punti strategici del nemico per debilitarne la capacità offensiva.

La campagna terrestre propriamente detta non iniziò fino a che l'alto comando della coalizione determinò che si presentavano le condizioni favorevoli. L'attacco fu una vera e propria opera d'arte della strategia, ideata dal generale nordamericano Norman Schwarzkopf e dal suo stato maggiore. Dopo aver disposto di fronte alle coste del Kuwait una considerevole forza di Marine per far credere agli iraqeni l'imminenza di uno sbarco, l'esercito procedette fiancheggiando le truppe di Saddam Hussein da ovest, attraverso il deserto dello stesso Iraq, tagliando in questo modo le vie di rifornimento delle truppe d'occupazione situate in Kuwait. L'attacco fu fulminante: in soli 4 giorni tutto era concluso. Più di 100.000 soldati iraqeni si resero in massa, lasciando dietro di sè migliaia di morti di fronte a solamente dei pochi tra le forze della coalizione. Il concetto della guerra era cambiato.

⊙

「砂漠の嵐」作戦とは、一般的に、1991年2月24日から28日まで、クウェートがその1年前にイラクに占領されたことにより、多国籍軍が決行したクウェート解放のために行われた地上作戦のことを指します。多国籍軍は、国連の決定により、アメリカを主導として31の国々の参加により構成され、開戦当初は、イラクの軍事基地などを中心に爆撃を行うことによって、その戦力を弱めることを目的にしていました。

「砂漠の嵐」作戦は、多国籍軍が戦局を優位に持っていくまでは決行されませんでした。この作戦は、当時のアメリカ軍の中でも天才的な頭脳をもつと言われていた中央軍司令官ノーマン・シュワルツコフが中心となって考案した戦略でした。クウェートの海岸部に多国籍海軍の多くを集めることによって、緊迫していたイラク軍にそれら海軍の上陸を信じさせ、サダム・フセインの軍隊をイラクの砂漠、西側に導いて攻撃することで、クウェートを占領したいたイラク軍の補給路を断つ、というのが目的でした。多国籍軍による攻撃は集中的に行われ、その結果、この作戦は4日間で終結を迎えました。100,000人以上のイラク軍兵士が降伏したのに対し、多国籍軍は、わずかの犠牲者を出しただけでした。この戦争はいろいろな面で、現代における戦争の仕方がそれまでの戦争の仕方と違うことを世界に示しました。

fra ⓘ Article Wikipèdia

ita ⓘ Articolo Wikipedia

jap ⓘ ウィキペディアの記事

by US Armed Forces

1991 Desert Storm
Middle East – Gulf War

Por lo general la denominación "Tormenta del Desierto" hace referencia a las operaciones terrestres llevadas a cabo entre el 24 y el 28 de febrero de 1991 por la coalición internacional para devolver la soberanía a Kuwait, invadida por Irak un año antes. La coalición, compuestas por 31 países y liderada por los EEUU bajo mandato de la ONU, inició los ataques con una larga serie de bombardeos a puntos estratégicos del enemigo para debilitar su capacidad ofensiva.

La campaña terrestre propiamente dicha no comenzó hasta que el alto mando de la coalición determinó que se daban las condiciones favorables. El ataque fue un verdadero alarde de estrategia ideado por el general norteamericano Norman Schwarzkopf y su estado mayor. Tras disponer frente a las costas de Kuwait a una importante fuerza de Marines para hacer creer a los iraquíes en la inminencia de un desembarco, procedió a flanquear a las tropas de Saddam Hussein por el oeste, por el propio desierto de Irak, y cortar así las vías de suministros de las tropas de ocupación en Kuwait. El ataque fue fulminante, en tan sólo 4 días todo había terminado. Más de 100.000 soldados iraquíes se rindieron en masa, dejando atrás miles de muertos frente a tan sólo unos pocos de la coalición. El concepto de guerra había cambiado.

Generally the name "Desert Storm" makes reference to terrestrial operations carried out between February 24 and 28, 1991, on the part of the international coalition in order to give back sovereignty to Kuwait, invaded by Iraq a year before. The coalition, comprised of 31 countries, and led by the United States under the UN command, started the attack by bombing strategic enemy spots in order to weaken its offensive capacity.

The terrestrial campaign itself did not start until the coalition's high command decided that there were favourable conditions. The attack was a real showing-off strategy, created by the North American general Norman Schwarzfkopf and his staff. After locating important Marines forces in front of Kuwait coasts, in order to make the Iraqis believe in the imminence of a disembarkation, started to flank Saddam Hussein's troops on the West, along Iraq's desert itself, cutting thus the occupation troops supply routes in Kuwait. The attack was overwhelming, only four days and everything had ended. More than 100,000 Iraqi soldiers surrendered massively, leaving behind thousands of casualties, the coalition lost only a few. War concept had changed.

Im Allgemeinen bezieht sich die Bezeichnung „Sandsturm" auf die Bodenoperationen, die zwischen dem 24. und 28. Februar 1991 durch die internationale Koalition vorgenommen wurden, um Kuwait von der Besetzung durch den Irak zu befreien, die ein Jahr vorher stattgefunden hatte. Die Koalition bestand aus 31. Ländern und wurde von den USA unter UNO-Mandat angeführt. Die Angriffe begannen mit einer langen Reihe von Bombardierungen strategischer Punkte, um die Angriffskapazität des Feindes zu schwächen.

Die Bodenkampagne selbst begann, als die Führung der Koalition feststellte, dass die Umstände günstig waren. Der Angriff war ein strategisches Meisterstück, ausgeklügelt von dem nordamerikanischen General Norman Schwarzkopf und seinem Generalstab. Vor der Küste Kuwaits wurde Marine in großer Zahl stationiert, damit die Iraker an eine bevorstehende Landung glaubten. Danach wurden die Truppen Saddam Husseins vom Westen, von der irakischen Küste aus flankiert, um so den Besatzungstruppen in Kuwait die Versorgung abzuschneiden. Es war ein Blitzangriff. In nur 4 Tagen war alles vorbei. Mehr als 100.000 irakische Soldaten ergaben sich und hinterließen tausende von Toten gegenüber einigen wenigen Gefallenen der Koalition. Das Konzept des Krieges hatte sich geändert.

esp · Artículo Wikipedia

eng · Wikipedia Article

deu · Wikipedia-Artikel

DESERT STORM

1991

This is England

by Apcbg

by British Army

REPÚBLICA ARGENTINA
1982
2007
LA NACIÓN A SUS HÉROES

MALVINAS ARGENTINAS
2 DE ABRIL
1982
2 PESOS
2007

ROYAL MARINES MUSEUM

ALL WELCOME

FREE ACCESS TO SHOP & TEA ROOM
WITHOUT ADMISSION TO THE MUSEUM

© Richard Lewis

by US Navy

Dans les confins de l'hémisphère sud, très près de la Terre du Feu, a éclaté une des guerres les plus controversées du XXe siècle. Le général Leopoldo Galtieri, président de l'Assemblée militaire qui gouvernait l'Argentine en 1982, décide d'envahir les Îles Malouines, de souveraineté britannique, pour dévier l'attention politique face à l'opposition croissante à la dictature. Le Royaume-Uni, après plusieurs tentatives de négociation, envoie une force aéronavale considérable pour aider ses troupes dans la récupération des îles.

Le 21 mai, à l'aube, les forces spéciales britanniques débarquent sur la baie de San Carlos sous un harcèlement intense de l'aviation argentine. Une semaine plus tard, le 2ᵉ de Parachutiste prend à l'assaut la base aérienne de Goose Green (La Prairie de l'oie), située dans le stratégique isthme qui divisait en deux l'Île Soledad. Ce fut la première et la plus importante bataille terrestre de la guerre. Les combats cruels qui se sont déroulés là se sont soldés avec près de 170 disparitions et plus de mille prisonniers argentins. Du côté britannique, 80 disparus, dont le colonel H. Jones, chef de la 2ᵉ de Parachutistes, décoré posthumément avec la Croix Victoria. La voie pour occuper la capitale des Malouines, Stanley, était ouverte et avec elle la fin de la guerre.

Ai confini dell'emisfero sud, vicino alla Terra del Fuoco, ebbe luogo una delle guerre più polemiche del XX secolo. Il generale Leopoldo Galtieri, presidente della Giunta Militare che governava l'Argentina nel 1982, decise di invadere le Isole Malvine, sotto sovranità britannica, per deviare l'attenzione pubblica di fronte alla crescente opposizione alla dittatura. Il Regno Unito, dopo vari tentativi di negoziazione, inviò una considerevole forza aeronavale per appoggiare le proprie truppe nel recupero delle isole.

All'alba del 21 maggio le forze speciali britanniche iniziarono lo sbarco nella baia di San Carlos, sotto un intenso attacco da parte dell'aviazione argentina. Una settimana più tardi, il 2° Paracadutisti prese d'assalto la base aerea di Goose Green (la Prateria dell'Oca), situata nello strategico istmo che divide in due l'Isola Soledad. Era la prima e la più importante battaglia di questa guerra. I cruenti combattimenti che vi ebbero luogo si saldarono con 170 vittime e oltre mille prigionieri argentini. Da parte britannica, ci furono 80 vittime, tra cui il colonnello H. Jones, capo del 2° Paracadutisti, cui si assegnò la decorazione postuma della Croce Vittoria. Il cammino per occupare la capitale delle Malvine, Stanley, era aperto e con esso la fine della guerra.

南半球の彼方、フエゴ諸島の近くで、20世紀の戦争の中でも最も多くの問題を抱えた戦争が起こりました。1982年、アルゼンチン陸軍司令官で大統領であったレオポルド・ガルチェリは、当時イギリス領であったマルビーナス諸島（フォークランド諸島）を占領することを決めました。これは、アルゼンチン国内でのガルチェリの独裁政権に対する反対の気運が高まっていたのをそらすためでした。そして、これに対してイギリスは、何回か交渉を試みましたが決着が着かなかったため、この島々を奪回するために空軍と海軍の兵士を送ることにしました。

同年の5月21日の明け方、イギリス軍は、アルゼンチン空軍の攻撃を受けながらも、サン・カルロス湾に上陸を始めました。その1週間後、イギリス軍のパラシュート部隊第2団が、グース・グリーン空軍基地（ラ・パラデラ・デル・ガンソ）に降下しました。ここは、ソレダッド島を二つに分ける重要な地峡でした。この戦いは、フォークランド紛争の一連の戦いの中でも特に激しいもので、結果として、アルゼンチン軍の兵士およそ170人が死亡、1,000人以上が捕虜になり、イギリス軍は80人の兵士が死亡し、その中には、第2パラシュート部隊隊長のH.ジョーンズ中佐も含まれていました。この中佐には後、勝利の十字架が送られました。そして、フォークランド諸島の首都、スタンレーはイギリス軍に占領され、この戦争に終わりが告げられました。

fra ⓘ Article Wikipèdia

ita ⓘ Articolo Wikipedia

jap ⓘ ウィキペディアの記事

1982 Goose Green
South Atlantic – The Falklands War

En el confín del hemisferio sur, muy cerca de la Tierra de Fuego, tuvo lugar una de las guerras más polémicas del siglo XX. El general Leopoldo Galtieri, presidente de la Junta Militar que gobernaba Argentina en 1982, decide invadir las Islas Malvinas, de soberanía británica, para desviar la atención política ante la creciente oposición a la dictadura. El Reino Unido, tras varios intentos de negociación, envía una considerable fuerza aeronaval para apoyar a sus tropas en la recuperación de las islas.

En la madrugada del 21 de mayo las fuerzas especiales británicas inician el desembarco en la bahía de San Carlos bajo un intenso acoso de la aviación argentina. Una semana después, el 2º de Paracaidistas toma por asalto la base aérea de Goose Green (la Pradera del Ganso), ubicada en el estratégico istmo que dividía en dos la Isla Soledad. Era la primera y más relevante batalla terrestre de la guerra. Los cruentos combates que allí tuvieron lugar se saldaron con unas 170 bajas y más de mil prisioneros argentinos. Por parte británica 80 bajas, entre ellas el teniente coronel H. Jones, jefe del 2º de Paracaidistas, condecorado póstumamente con la Cruz Victoria. El camino para ocupar la capital de las Malvinas, Stanley, estaba abierto y con ello el final de la guerra.

Where the southern hemisphere comes to an end, close to Tierra del Fuego, one of the most polemic wars of the twentieth century took place. General Leopoldo Galtieri, president of the Military Junta, governing Argentina in 1982, decides to invade the Falkland Islands, of British sovereignty, in order to distract political attention on the increasing opposition to the dictatorship. The United Kingdom, after several negotiation intents, sends considerable air and sea forces to support its troops in order to recover the islands.

Very early in the morning, on May 21, the special British troops start disembarking in San Carlos Bay, under intense attack on the part of the Argentinean air force. A week later, the Second Paratrooper regiment assaults Goose Green air base, located at the strategic isthmus which divides Soledad Island in two. It was the first and most relevant land battle of the war. Cruel combats which took place there resulted in 170 casualties and more than a thousand Argentinean prisoners. On the British side there were 80 casualties, among them the Lieutenant-Colonel H. Jones, Chief of the 2nd. Paratroopers Regiment; the Victoria Cross was bestowed on him posthumously. The way for the occupation of Stanley, the Falklands capital, was open; this meant that the war was over.

An der Grenze der südlichen Hemisphäre, ganz in der Nähe von Feuerland fand einer der umstrittensten Kriege des zwanzigsten Jahrhunderts statt. Der General Leopoldo Galtieri, Präsident der Militärjunta, die 1982 in Argentinien an der Macht war, beschließt die Falklandinseln einzunehmen, die damals in britischer Hand waren, um die politische Aufmerksamkeit von der wachsenden Opposition gegen die Diktatur abzulenken. Das Vereinigte Königreich schickt nach mehreren Versuchen der Verhandlung eine beachtliche Truppe zur Verstärkung der Wiedereroberungstruppen auf den Inseln.

Am frühen Morgen des 21. März beginnen die britischen Spezialeinheiten die Landung in der Bucht San Carlos unter schweren Angriffen der argentinischen Luftwaffe. Eine Woche später nimmt die 2. Division der Fallschirmspringer die Basis von Goose Green ein, die sich auf dem strategischen Isthmus befindet, der die Insel Soledad in zwei Teile teilt. Es war die erste und wichtigste Bodenschlacht des Kriegs. Die harten Kämpfe hatten 170 Tote und mehr als tausend argentinische Gefangene zur Folge. Auf britischer Seite gab es 80 Tote, unter ihnen der Oberstleutnant H. Jones, der die 2. Division der Fallschirmspringer leitete und posthum mit dem Victory-Kreuz ausgezeichnet wurde. Der Weg zur Hauptstadt der Falklandinseln, Stanley, war offen und somit der Krieg beendet.

esp · Artículo Wikipedia

eng · Wikipedia Article

deu · Wikipedia-Artikel

GOOSE GREEN

1982

NICARAGUA · 1912 ⭑ VERA · CRUZ · 1914 ⭑ HAITI · 1915 – 1934 ⭑ SANTO · DOMINGO · 1916 – 192
– 1991 ⭑ PANAMA · 1988 – 1990 ·

DIAN · WARS · 1835 – 1842 ⭑

The Lost Evidence

REVOLUTIONARY·WAR·1775–1783 ★ FRENCH·NAVAL·WAR·1798–1801 ★ TRIPOLI·1801–1805 ★ WAR·OF·1812–1815

1945 IWO JIMA·OKINAWA·KOREA·1950·

UNCOMMON
VALOR
WAS A COMMON
VIRTUE

FIDELIS

by Anne Dayton

Flags over Iwo Jima

Tadamichi Kuribayashi

Lt. G. Holland M. Smith

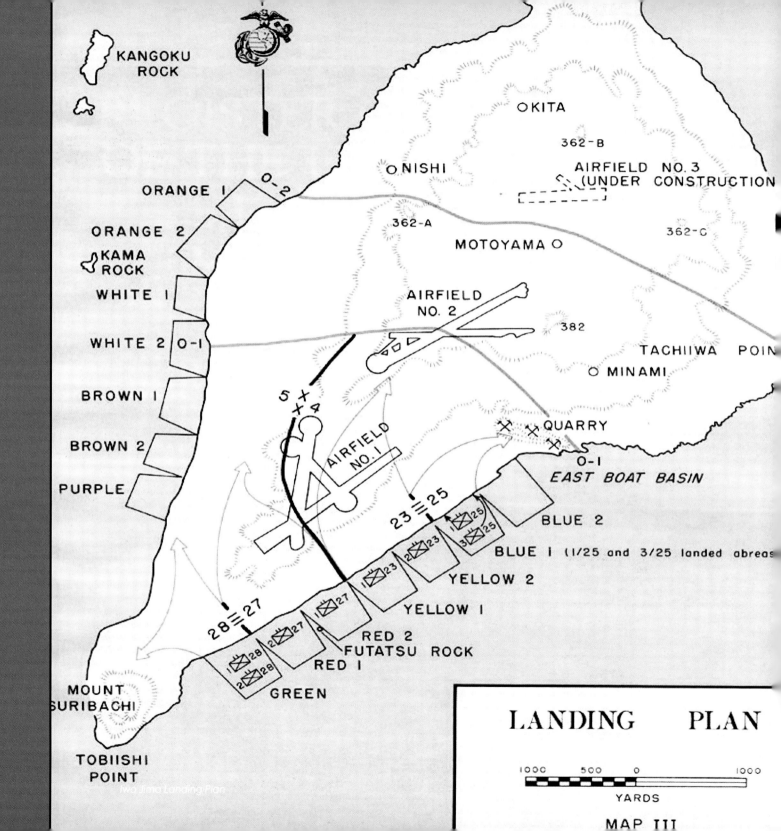

KANGOKU
ROCK

OKITA

362-B

ONISHI

AIRFIELD NO. 3
(UNDER CONSTRUCTION)

362-A

362-C

ORANGE 1 O-2

MOTOYAMA O

ORANGE 2

KAMA
ROCK

AIRFIELD
NO. 2

382

WHITE 1

WHITE 2 O-1

TACHIIWA POIN

O MINAMI

BROWN 1

5 X
X 4

BROWN 2

QUARRY

AIRFIELD
NO. I

O-1

PURPLE

EAST BOAT BASIN

23 ≡ 25

1 X 25

BLUE 2

3 X 25

2 X 23

BLUE I (1/25 and 3/25 landed abreas

1 X 23

YELLOW 2

YELLOW I

28 ≡ 27

1 X 27

RED 2

2 X 27

FUTATSU ROCK

1 X 28

RED I

2 X 28

GREEN

MOUNT
SURIBACHI

TOBIISHI
POINT

Iwo Jima Landing Plan

LANDING   PLAN

1000   500   0   1000

YARDS

MAP III

Iwo Jima est une petite ville volcanique de l'archipel d'Ogasawara à 1 200 km au sud de Tokyo. De prime abord, personne ne peut comprendre comment une île stérile a pu devenir la scène d'une bataille sanglante. L'importance stratégique de cette enclave japonaise reposait sur son radar et champs d'aviation, qui rendaient plus difficile et avertissaient du passage des bombardiers de longue portée nord-américains en direction de Tokyo.

Le haut commandement japonais, conscient de la fin de la guerre, cherchait la manière d'atteindre une paix honorable. Il s'est dit alors que s'il rendait le plus difficile possible la conquête de n'importe laquelle de ses îles, les États-Unis n'occuperaient pas le Japon, craignant une grande saignée entre ses troupes. Cela a eu des conséquences imprévisibles. Loin d'une paix honorable, la drastique décision est prise de lancer la bombe atomique.

Même si le débarquement des Marines et la conquête du Mont Subirachi (rendu célèbre par les photographies de Rosenthal du hissage du drapeau) ont été relativement rapides, la conquête de l'île d'Iwo Jima a duré plus d'un mois. Les troupes japonaises se sont retranchées dans des bunkers, des fossés et des tunnels impénétrables. Et la presque totalité des plus de 20 000 combattants ont perdu la vie.

Iwo Jima è una piccola isola vulcanica dell'arcipelago di Ogasawara, a 1.200 km al sud di Tokio. A prima vista, nessuno potrebbe comprendere come un'isola sterile sia potuta diventare lo scenario di una sanguinosa battaglia. L'importanza strategica di quest'enclave giapponese radicava nel suo radar e nei suoi campi aeronautici che ostacolavano il passaggio dei bombardieri statunitensi a lungo raggio e avvertivano della loro presenza sulla rotta verso Tokio.

L'alto comando giapponese, ormai conscio dell'esito della guerra, cercava il modo di raggiungere una pace decorosa. Pensò quindi che, se avesse potuto ostacolare al massimo la conquista di una qualsiasi delle proprie isole, gli USA non occuperebbero il Giappone, temendo che le proprie truppe venissero decimate. Ma questa decisione ebbe invece delle conseguenze imprevisibili: ben lungi dall'idea della pace decorosa, gli USA presero la decisione di sganciare la bomba atomica.

Sebbene lo sbarco dei Marine e la conquista del Monte Subirachi (famoso per le fotografie scattate da Rosenthal ai militari che issavano la bandiera statunitense) siano stati relativamente veloci, la conquista dell'isola di Iwo Jima durò più di un mese. Le truppe giapponesi si trincerarono in bunker, fossi e tunnel impenetrabili, e quasi tutti i 20.000 combattenti persero la vita.

硫黄島は、東京から南方に1,200キロ下ったところにある小笠原諸島を構成する火山島のひとつです。太平洋に浮かぶこの小さな不毛の島を見ていると、どうしてここが、日米大戦の重要な戦場のひとつになったのかわからないかもしれません。しかし、この南海の孤島は、アメリカ軍の日本攻撃のための長距離爆撃機の到来を知らせたり、爆撃機の本土到達を困難にするために、戦略的に非常に重要な場所にありました。

日本の政府や大本営の中では、幹部たちはこの時期になると、日本の勝利は不可能であるから、少なくとも威厳を保ちつつ平和裡に終戦を迎える方法を検討していました。そのため、アメリカ軍の日本本土への攻撃をなるべく遅らせることによって、アメリカ軍の日本占領を避け、日本の損傷を最小限に留めようとしましたが、最終的には、これらの考えとは程遠い終戦の方法、「原子爆弾」が落とされることによって日米戦争が終結したのでした。もっとも、この当時の日本の政治家や軍人の中で、この破壊的な結果を想像できた人はおそらくいませんでした。

硫黄島の戦いは、この島でアメリカ軍の威力を弱めることを目的にその準備が徹底されました。そのため、アメリカ軍海軍が上陸し、摺鉢山に星条旗を掲げた後も（映画や記録写真で知られている場面）、日本軍の抵抗は1ヶ月以上も続きました。日本軍は、トーチカ（または「特火点」と呼ばれる鉄筋コンクリートの防御施設）や塹壕、何十キロにも渡って掘られたトンネルを巧みに使用してアメリカ軍の攻撃に絶えましたが、壮絶な戦いの結果、最終的に20,000人もの日本軍兵士が亡くなりました。

fra ⓘ Article Wikipèdia

ita ⓘ Articolo Wikipedia

jap ⓘ ウィキペディアの記事

by Louis R. Lowery

1945 Iwo Jima
North West Pacific – World War II

Iwo Jima es una pequeña isla volcánica del archipiélago de Ogasawara a 1.200 km al sur de Tokio. A primera vista nadie puede llegar a entender cómo una estéril isla pudo llegar a convertirse en el escenario de una sangrienta batalla. La importancia estratégica de este enclave japonés radicaba en su radar y campos de aviación que dificultaban y advertían del paso de los bombarderos de largo alcance norteamericanos rumbo a Tokio.

El alto mando japonés consciente del final de la guerra buscaba la forma de alcanzar una paz honrosa. Pensó entonces que si dificultaba los máximo posible la conquista de cualquiera de sus islas, los EEUU no ocuparían Japón temerosos de una gran sangría entre sus tropas. Esto tuvo unas consecuencias impredecibles, lejos de una paz honrosa, se toman la drástica decisión de lanzar la bomba atómica.

Aunque el desembarco de los Marines y la conquista del Monte Subirachi (famoso por las fotografías de Rosenthal del alzamiento de la bandera) fueron relativamente rápidos, la conquista de la isla de Iwo Jima duró más de un mes. Las tropas japonesas se atrincheraron en búnkeres, fosos y túneles impenetrables, perdiendo la vida la casi totalidad de los más de 20.000 combatientes.

Iwo Jima is a little volcanic island of the Ogasawara archipielago, 1200 km south of Tokio. At first sight nobody can understand why a desert island could become the scenario of a bloody battle. The strategic importance of this Japanese spot, had to do with its radar and with aviation fields which rendered difficult for long reach bombers their passing toward Tokio warning about their presence.

The Japanese high command, aware of the end of the war, tried to reach an honourable peace. They thought that if they could render extremely difficult the conquest of any of their islands, the United States would not occupy Japan, fearful of a great bleeding among their troops. This had unpredictable consequences, very far from an honoured peace; the unpredictable decision of launching the atomic bomb was taken.

Though the Marines disembarkation and the conquest of Mount Subirachi (famous for Rosenthal's photos about the flag raising) where relatively fast, Iwo Jima island conquest lasted more than a month. Japanese troops entrenched in bunkers, pits and impenetrable tunnels. Most of them died, they were more than 20,000.

Iwo Jima ist eine kleine Vulkaninsel des Archipiels Ogasawara 1.200 km südlich von Tokio. Auf den ersten Blick kann keiner verstehen, wie eine sterile Insel sich in Schauplatz eines blutigen Kampfes verwandeln kann. Diese japanische Enklave war aufgrund des Radars und der Flugfelder strategisch wichtig, die den Flug der nordamerikanischen Bomber mit Kurs auf Tokio erschwerten und diese ausfindig machten.

Die japanische Führung war sich des Kriegsendes bewusst und suchte einen Weg zu einem ehrenvollen Frieden. Man dachte, wenn man die Eroberung jeder noch so kleinen Insel möglichst erschwerte, würden die USA Japan nicht besetzen, da sie sich vor einem Gemetzel fürchteten. Die Folgen waren unvorhersehbar. Weit entfernt von einem ehrenvollen Frieden beschließt man den Abwurf der Atombombe.

Obwohl die Landung der Marine und die Eroberung des Bergs Subirachi (berühmt aufgrund der Photos von Rosenthal mit dem Hissen der Fahne) relativ schnell vonstatten gingen, dauerte die Eroberung der Insel Iwo Jima mehr als einen Monat. Die japanischen Truppen verschanzten sich in Bunkern, Gräben und undurchdringlichen Tunnel. Fast alle 20.000 Kämpfende verloren ihr Leben.

esp ℹ Artículo Wikipedia

eng ℹ Wikipedia Article

deu ℹ Wikipedia-Artikel

IWO JIMA

1945

В ДОМЕ
ЭТОМ
СЛИЛИСЬ
ВОЕДИНО
ПОДВИГ
РАТНЫЙ И
ТРУДОВОЙ

ОТСТОИМ ТЕБЯ
РОДНОЙ
СТАЛИНГРАД!

© Andrey Volykhov

Memorial

Entre le fer et le ciment, les rues et les ruines, s'est tenu la Bataille urbaine la plus connue de toute l'histoire. Aux rives de la Volga, dans la frontière orientale de l'Europe, la ville de Stalingrad rebaptisée en honneur du leader soviétique (aujourd'hui Volgograd), avait été transformée par Staline en une importante ville industrielle et un noyau de communications. Pour l'armée allemande, il s'agissait d'un objectif supplémentaire de l'opération « Fall Blau » avec laquelle elle prétendait occuper les puits pétroliers du Caucase et obtenir ainsi du carburant pour ses chars de combat.

Par excès de confiance, Hitler décide de diviser les forces attaquantes, en laissant au VIe armée du Général Von Paulus seul face à la défense acharnée russe qui en plus de freiner l'avancée de l'ennemi finira par le cerner. Entre juin 1942 et février 1943 se produit un véritable massacre où ont eu lieu de cruels combats pour n'obtenir qu'une rue ou qu'un bâtiment.

Ce fut la bataille des francs-tireurs qui, cachés entre les décombres, assassinaient avec une totale impunité; l'on était sûr nulle part, c'était la dénommée « guerre des rats ». Le nombre de vies perdues fut accablant : environ 750 000 disparitions du côté allemand et le même nombre pour les forces russes et plus d'un million de civils morts, les véritables victimes de la guerre.

Tra ferro e cemento, tra strade e rovine, si sviluppò una delle più famose battaglie urbane della storia. Sulle rive del Volga e sul confine orientale dell'Europa, la città di Stalingrado, ribattezzata in onore del leader sovietico (oggi Volgograd), era stata trasformata da Stalin in un importante centro industriale e nodo delle vie di comunicazione. Per l'esercito tedesco si trattava semplicemente di un ulteriore obiettivo nell'ambito dell'operazione "Fall Blau", con la quale intendeva occupare i pozzi petroliferi del Caucaso ed ottenere in questo modo il combustibile necessario per i propri carri armati.

Sottovalutando la situazione, Hitler decise di dividere le forze d'attacco lasciando il VI Esercito del generale von Paulus solo davanti alla ferrea difesa russa, che oltre a frenare l'avanzata nemica lo terminò circondando. Tra il giugno del 1942 e il febbraio del 1943, si produce un vero e proprio massacro, in cui ebbero luogo cruenti combattimenti al solo scopo di conquistare una strada o un edificio.

Quella di Stalingrado fu anche la battaglia dei cecchini che, nascosti tra i resti, assassinavano nella più completa impunità; nella cosiddetta "guerra dei topi", nessuno era al sicuro, in nessun posto. Il bilancio della battaglia fu devastante: circa 750.000 vittime da parte tedesca, altrettante tra le forze russe, con oltre un milione di morti tra i civili, le vere vittime della guerra.

戦史に残る数多くの市街戦の中でも、このスターリングラードの戦いは史上最大の攻防戦となり、莫大な数の犠牲者を出したことで知られています。第二次世界大戦当時、ヴォルガ川はヨーロッパ東部の境とソビエト時代のロシアの間を流れていました。そしてスターリングラードの町（現在はヴォルゴグラード）は、産業と情報網の中心地として、スターリンの名前を付けられました。ドイツ軍にとっては、この戦いは、「ブラウ作戦」の一環として軍隊の燃料を供給するため油田の確保を目的にしたもので、それ以上の「不必要な戦い」は望んでいませんでした。

その上ヒトラーは、ドイツ軍の勢力を過信していたので、攻撃用の兵士を分けることにし、フォン・パウルス大将の第6軍のみを前線に残しました。一方のソ連軍は、それらドイツ軍の前進を食い止めるだけでなく、結果的には敵軍を包囲する形になりました。そして、1942年の6月から1943年の2月まで、スターリングラードの町は戦場と化しました。ドイツ軍、ソ連軍とも、1つの建物、一本の通り、1本の地下壕を占拠するまで戦い、廃墟となったそれらの施設までも「要塞」として使用しました。

このスターリングラードの戦いは、狙撃兵が非常に活躍したことでも知られています。狙撃兵たちは、瓦礫の後ろに隠れ、あらゆるものに対して容赦なくその銃口を向けました。そのため、この町ではどこにいても誰も安全ではなく、のちに「ネズミ戦争」と呼ばれるようになりました。この史上稀に見る残酷な戦いの結果、ドイツ軍は750,000人の兵士が死亡、ソ連軍もほぼ同数の死亡者を出し、そして、真の戦争被害者である一般市民は、百万人以上が犠牲になったと言われています。

fra 🛈 Article Wikipèdia

ita 🛈 Articolo Wikipedia

jap 🛈 ウィキペディアの記事

flickr © dodgydago

Medal defense of Stalingrad
© Grafikm fr

Bloodiest Battle

1942 Stalingrad
East Europe – World War II

Entre hierro y cemento, calles y ruinas se desarrolló la más conocida batalla urbana de la historia. A orillas del Volga, en la frontera oriental de Europa, la ciudad de Stalingrado rebautizada en honor al líder soviético (hoy Volgogrado), había sido convertida por Stalin en una importante ciudad industrial y nudo de comunicaciones. Para el ejército alemán se trataba de un objetivo más de la operación "Fall Blau" con la que pretendía ocupar los pozos petrolíferos del Cáucaso y obtener así combustible para sus carros de combate.

En un exceso de confianza Hitler decide dividir las fuerzas atacantes, dejando al VI Ejército del general von Paulus sólo ante la férrea defensa rusa que además de frenar el avance enemigo acabará cercándolo. Entre junio de 1942 a febrero de 1943 se produce una verdadera masacre en la que tuvieron lugar cruentos combates para tan sólo obtener una calle o un edificio.

Fue también la batalla de los francotiradores que, ocultos entre los restos, asesinaban con total impunidad; nadie podía estaba seguro en ningún sitio, era la denominada "guerra de las ratas". El saldo en vidas fue abrumador: unas 750.000 bajas del bando alemán, otro tanto de las fuerzas rusas y más de un millón de civiles muertos, las verdaderas víctimas de la guerra.

Among iron and mortar, streets and ruins, the most renowned human battle of the history took place. By the Volga, on the East European frontier, the city of Stalingrad, renamed in honour of the soviet leader (nowadays Volgograde), had been converted by Stalin in an important industrial city and communication centre. For the German army it was one of the goals of the "Fall Blau" operation with which they intended to occupy the Caucasian oil wells, obtaining in that way fuel for their combat cars.

Excessively self-confident Hitler decides to split the enemy forces, leaving general von Paulus' VI Army alone in the presence of the iron Russian defence which apart from detaining the enemy's advance, ends surrounding it. Between June 1942 and February 1943 a real massacre takes place where cruel combats occurred only to obtain a street or a building.

It was also the snipers' battle who, hidden among the remains, killed with total impunity; nobody could be safe in any place, it was the so called "war of the rats". Lives loss was overwhelming: about 70,000 victims on the German side, a similar amount on the Russian forces and more than a million of dead civilians, the real war victims.

Zwischen Stahl und Zement, Straßen und Ruinen fand die bekannteste Stadtschlacht der Geschichte statt. Am Wolgaufer, an der Ostgrenze Europas war die Stadt Stalingrad, die zu Ehren des sovietischen Führers umgenannt worden war (heute Wolgograd), von Stalin in eine wichtige Industriestadt und Kommunikationsknoten verwandelt. Für das deutsche Heer handelte es sich um ein weiteres Ziel der Operation „Fall Blau", mit dem man die Erdölbohrungen des Kaukausus besetzen wollte, um so Treibstoff für die Panzer zu erhalten.

Hitler überschätzte sich und beschloss, die angreifenden Kräfte zu teilen, wodurch das 6. Heer des Generals von Paulus sich der eisernen russischen Verteidigung allein gegenübersah, die den Feind nicht nur aufhielt sondern auch einkesselte. Zwischen Juni 1942 und Februar 1943 entwickelt sich ein echte Massakers, in dessen Verlauf um eine einzige Straße oder ein einziges Gebäude grausame Schlachten geschlagen wurden.

Es war auch die Schlacht der Freischützen, die, verborgen zwischen den Trümmern, ungestraft mordeten; niemand war irgendwo sicher, es war der sogenannte „Rattenkrieg". Die Zahl der Opfer war überwältigend: 750.000 Tote auf deutscher Seite, die selbe Anzahl bei den russischen Truppen und mehr als eine Million tote Zivilisten, die wirklichen Opfer des Kriegs.

esp ⓘ Artículo Wikipedia

eng ⓘ Wikipedia Article

deu ⓘ Wikipedia-Artikel

STALINGRAD

1942

El Alamein 5/5

El Alamein 4/5

Rommels Frühjahrsoffensive 1941

Rommel war nicht bereit, sich auf eine bewegliche Verteidigung zu beschränken, und er schob seine 5. leichte Division bis zur Enge von Marsa el Brega vor. Entgegen den Vorstellungen von Rom und Berlin befahl er am 31. März den Angriff. Bei den Briten, die durch d... ... und geschwächt waren, entwickelte sich bald eine ... ...loß sich Rommel zu dem Versuch, die ganze Cyre... ...els einer Woche gelang.

... ...e Cyrenaica bis zur Westlichen Wüste (Ägypten),

...-Kristall- 1957 und Carell: Wüstenfüchse, S. 79 sowie Wolf Heckmann:

...VA DISPOSTO A LIMITARSI AD UNA DIFESA MOBILE E FECE AVANZARE LA SUA 5. A DIVISIONE LEGGERA FINO ALLA GOLA MARSA ELBREGA. IN CONTRASTO CON LE IDEEDI ROMA E DI BERLINO, ROMMEL IL 31 MARZO ORDINO DI ATTACCARE. BEN PRESTO PRESSO I BRITANNICI, INDEBOLITI DALLO SPOSTAMENTO DI TRUPPE VERSO LA GRECIA, LA SITUAZIONE SI FECE CRITICA. IL 3 APRILE ROMMEL DECISE DI TEHTARE DI CONQUISTARE TUTTA LA CIRENAICA. VI RIUSCI IN MENO DI UNA SETTIMANA.

CARTA: LA PRIMA AVANZATA DI ROMMEL IN CIRENAICA FINO AL DESERTO OCCIDENTALE (EGITTO), PRIMAVERA 1941

DISEGNO E.H.S. E EPPFLE (WGM) DA SKAF... "KRISTALL... WCSTE...

نظارة ميدان — غطاء رأس
كوفية خاصة بالقائد الألماني رومييل
Field Glass _ Cap
Havelock Belonging to field marshal **Rommel**

El Alamein 3/5

© Dominik Knippel

دبابة

سيرمان أمريكى

U.S.A general

sherman tank

General Bernard L. Montgomery watches his tanks move up, North Africa, November 1942.

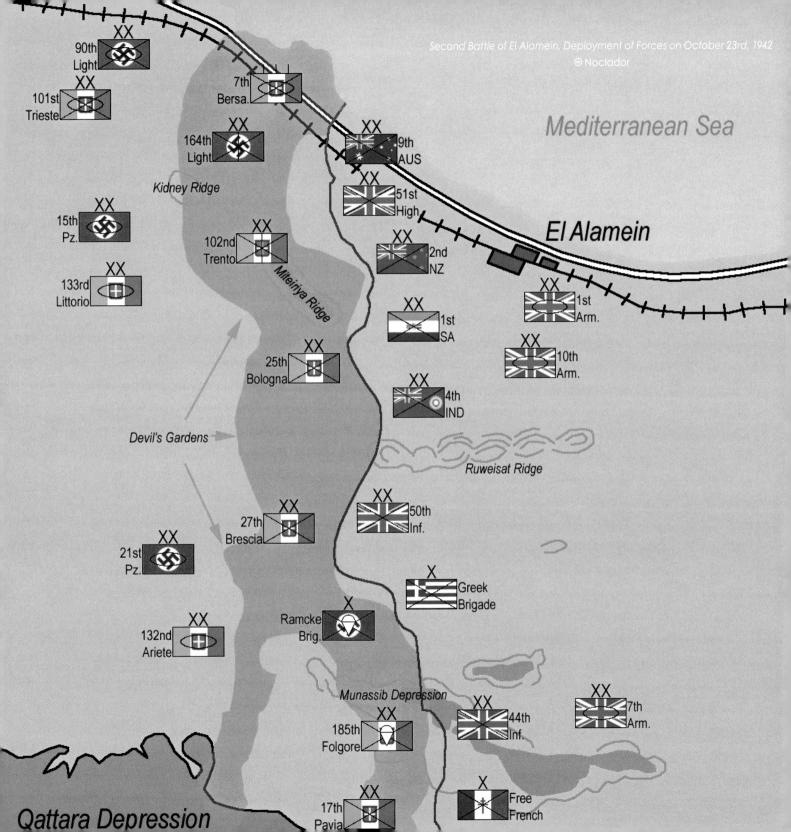

Second Battle of El Alamein, Deployment of Forces on October 23rd, 1942
© Noclador

Mediterranean Sea

El Alamein

90th
Light

101st
Trieste

7th
Bersa.

164th
Light

9th
AUS

51st
High

Kidney Ridge

15th
Pz.

102nd
Trento

133rd
Littorio

Miteiriya Ridge

2nd
NZ

1st
SA

1st
Arm.

10th
Arm.

25th
Bologna

4th
IND

Devil's Gardens

Ruweisat Ridge

27th
Brescia

50th
Inf.

21st
Pz.

Greek
Brigade

132nd
Ariete

Ramcke
Brig.

Munassib Depression

44th
Inf.

7th
Arm.

185th
Folgore

17th
Pavia

Free
French

Qattara Depression

flickr © David Holt

BADGE OF THE
GERMAN AFRIKA KORPS
"PANZER"

شعــار
الفيلق الأفريقى الألمانى
پــانــزر

El Alamein 2/5

El Alamein est le nom d'un petit village de la côte désertique du nord-ouest de l'Égypte. Ce fut le théâtre, entre le 1er et le 4 novembre 1942, des dénommées Première Bataille, Bataille d'Alam El Halfa et la Deuxième bataille d'El Alamein opposant l'Afrika Korps et la huitième Armée Britannique.

Après la libération de Tobrouk, les forces germano-italiennes commandées par le général Erwin Rommel, « le renard du désert », ont entrepris une avancée rapide par la côte méditerranéenne vers Le Caire dans la persécution de la Huitième armée commandée par le vétéran Sir Claude Auchinleck. Les alliés ont pris la décision de détenir la progression de l'Afrika Korps et de résister à leur poussée dans la zone d'El Alamein ce qui a donné lieu au premier combat. Auchinleck a été relevé de son poste par le général Montgomery qui a affronté les dernières tentatives d'avancée de Rommel à Alam El Halfa.

L'Afrika Korps sans à peine approvisionnement et exténués par autant de mois de combats incessants n'a pas pu supporter la contre-attaque de la Huitième Armée qui avait obtenu d'importants renforts. La Deuxième bataille d'El Alamein est devenue le point de retour définitif pour les forces de l'Axe qui battent en retraite et remontent jusqu'en Tunisie.

El Alamein è il nome di un paesino nella deserttica costa del nord-est egiziano. Li ebbero luogo tra l'1 di luglio e il 4 novembre del 1942 le così chiamate Prima Battaglia di El Alamein, Battaglia di Alam El Halfa e Seconda Battaglia di El Alamein, tra l'Afrika Korps e l'Ottavo Esercito britannico.

Dopo la liberazione di Tobruk, le forze italo-tedesche comandate dal generale Erwin Rommel, la "volpe del deserto", intrapresero una rapida avanzata lungo la costa mediterranea verso Il Cairo, inseguendo l'Ottavo Esercito comandato dal veterano generale Sir Claude Auchinleck. Gli alleati presero la decisione di arrestare l'avanzata dell'Afrika Korps e di resisterne le investite nella zona di El Alamein, dando luogo al primo scontro. Auchinleck fu rilevato dal suo posto dal generale Montgomery, che affrontò gli ultimi tentativi d'avanzata di Rommel ad Alam El Halfa.

L'Afrika Korps, quasi senza rifornimenti e sfinito dai tanti mesi di combattimenti incessanti, non potè sopportare il contrattacco dell'Ottavo Esercito che nel frattempo aveva ricevuto importanti rinforzi. La Seconda Battaglia di El Alamein diventò il definitivo punto di ritirata per le forze dell'Asse, che iniziarono un precipitoso ripiego fino alla Tunisia.

エル・アラメインは、エジプトの北西部の海岸部にある小さい村の名前です。この村で、1942年7月1日から11月4日まで、アフリカ軍団とイギリス軍第8機甲師団の間に激しい戦いが行われました。最初の戦いはアラム・エル・ファイファの戦いと呼ばれ、2回目の戦いはエル・アラメインの戦いと呼ばれています。トブルクの占領後、「砂漠の狐」と呼ばれたエルヴィン・ロンメル大将に率いられたドイツ・イタリアの枢軸国は、連合国軍総司令官のクルード・オーキンレックが指揮するイギリス軍第8機甲師団を追って、地中海沿岸をカイロ方面へと素早く移動しました。連合国軍は、アフリカ軍団の前進を阻止することを決め、エル・アラメインにおけるその勢力に対抗することにしました。その結果、最初の戦闘であるアラム・エル・ファイファの戦いが始まりました。オーキンレックは、その後、総司令官の地位をバーナート・モントゴメリーに譲りました。新しく第8機甲師団の指揮官に着任したモントゴメリーは、アラム・エル・ファルファにおけるロンメル大将の前進する動きに徹底的に交戦しました。。

アフリカ軍団は食料の補給も十分になく、何ヶ月も続く戦いからくる疲弊も重なり、兵力を補充することのできた連合国軍イギリス第8機甲師団の攻撃に耐えられなくなりました。エル・アラメインの戦いは、チュニジア方面へと急いで退却を始めた枢軸国にとって決定的な折り返し地点となり、その後北アフリカから全面的に撤退しました。

fra ⓘ Article Wikipèdia

ita ⓘ Articolo Wikipèdia

jap ⓘ ウィキペディアの記事

4468117 PRIVATE
T. HOLT
THE DURHAM LIGHT INFANTRY
2ND NOVEMBER 1942

El Alamein 1/5

1942 El Alamein
North Africa – World War II

El Alamein es el nombre de una pequeña población en la desértica costa del noroeste de Egipto. Allí tuvieron lugar entre el 1 de julio y el 4 de noviembre de 1942 las denominadas Primera Batalla, Batalla de Alam El Halfa y Segunda Batalla de El Alamein entre el Afrika Korps y el Octavo Ejército británico.

Tras la liberación de Tobruk, las fuerzas germano-italianas dirigidas por el general Erwin Rommel el "zorro del desierto", emprendieron un rápido avance por la costa mediterránea hacia El Cairo en persecución del Octavo Ejército comandado por el veterano general Sir Claude Auchinleck. Los aliados tomaron la decisión de detener el avance del Afrika Korps y resistir su empuje en la zona de El Alamein lo que dio lugar al primer combate. Auchinleck fue relevado de su puesto por el general Montgomery que se enfrentó a las últimas tentativas de avance de Rommel en Alam El Halfa.

El Afrika Korps sin apenas abastecimiento alguno y agotados por tantos meses de incesantes combates no pudo aguantar el contraataque del Octavo Ejército que había obtenido importantes refuerzos. La Segunda Batalla del Alamein se convirtió en el punto de retorno definitivo para las fuerzas del Eje que iniciaron una acelerada retirada hasta Túnez.

El Alamein is the name of a little village in the desert coast on the North East of Egypt. Between July 1 and November 4, 1942 the so called First Battle, Battle of Alam El Halfa and Second Battle of El Alamein, took place between the African Corps and the Eighth British Army.

After Tobruk liberation, the German–Italian forces, led by general Erwin Rommel "the desert fox", carried out a fast advance along the Mediterranean coast up to El Cairo, pursuing the Eight Army, led by the veteran general Sir Claude Auchinleck. The allies made the decision to stop the African Corps and to resist their pressure in El Alamein, which gave origin to the first combat. Auchinleck was relieved from his charge by general Montgomery who fought against the last Rommel's intents to advance in Alam El Halfa.

The African Corps without supplies and exhausted because of so many months of constant combats, could not resist the counterattack of the Eight Army which had got important reinforcements. The Second Battle of El Alamein became the final return point for the Axis forces, which started a fast retreat up to Tunisia.

El Alamein ist der Name einer kleinen Siedlung an der Nordwestküste Ägyptens. Dort fanden zwischen dem 1. Juli und dem 4. November 1942 die sogenannte Erste Schlacht, Schlacht des Alam El Halfa und Zweite Schlacht von El Alamein zwischen dem Afrika Korps und dem Achten Britischen Heer statt.

Nach der Befreiung von Tobruk unternahmen die deutsch-italienischen Truppen unter Führung des Generals Erwin Rommel, dem „Wüstenfuchs" einen schnellen Vorstoß an der Mittelmeerküste in Richtung Kairo, um das Achte Heer unter Führung des Veteranen Sir Claude Auchinleck zu verfolgen. Die Alliierten beschlossen, den Vormarsch des Afrika Korps zu stoppen und deren Vordringen in das Gebiet von El Alamein zu verhindern, wodurch es zu der ersten Schlacht kam. Auchinleck wurde durch den General Montgomery abgelöst, der den letzten Vorstoßversuchen von Rommel in Alam El Halfa Widerstand bot.

Das Afrika Korps war ohne Versorgung und durch monatelange Kämpfe zermürbt, wodurch es dem Gegenangriff des Achten Heeres nichts entgegenzusetzen hatte, das Unterstützung erhalten hatte. Die zweite Schlacht von Alamein wurde zum definitiven Rückzug für die Achsenmächte, die überstürzt Tunez zurückmarschierten.

esp ⓘ Artículo Wikipedia

eng ⓘ Wikipedia Article

deu ⓘ Wikipedia-Artikel

EL ALAMEIN

1942

© Sjwells53

MOUSSA DIARR

by Lt. J.W. Brooke

by British Official Photographer

by Lt. J.W. Brooke

by Lt. Ernest Brooks

Sous un champ fleuri de coquelicots se cachent aujourd'hui les restes d'une des batailles les plus sanglantes de la Grande Guerre, érigée en icône de la lutte infernale des tranchées. En 1916, la pression allemande sur les Français dans la zone de Verdun se faisait de plus en plus intense. Le haut commandement britannique décide alors de réaliser un mouvement de distraction en perçant les lignes ennemies dans la frontière franco-belge. Les conséquences ont été dévastatrices ; après six mois de durs combats et plus d'un million de disparus (dont 300 000 morts), l'avancée n'était que de 8km.

Entre les deux contingents, il existait une étendue de terrain appelée « no man's land » ou s'est succédé une infinité d'avancées et de retrait au prix d'innombrables pertes. Le premier jour d'assaut aux lignes allemandes, le 1er juillet sera rappelé comme le plus tragique de l'histoire de l'armée du Royaume-Uni, au cours duquel sont morts presque 20 000 soldats britanniques. Le manque de défense des troupes face à l'ennemi dans la fangeuse no man's land a conduit à l'introduction précipitée d'une nouvelle arme de combat, le char de combat, qui a été utilisé pour la première fois en Somme. Cette terrible bataille fut transmise à la postérité dans le premier reportage de guerre de l'Histoire.

Sotto un dolce manto di papaveri si nascondono oggi i resti di una delle battaglie più sanguinose della Grande Guerra, diventata l'icona dell'infernale lotta in trincea. Nel 1916 la pressione tedesca sui Francesi nella zona del Verdun si faceva sempre più intensa. L'alto comando britannico decise allora di realizzare un movimento di distrazione, rompendo le linee nemiche sul confine franco-belga. Le conseguenze furono devastanti: dopo sei mesi di duri combattimenti e oltre un milione di vittime (di cui 300.000 mortali) si era riusciti ad avanzare soltanto 8 km.

Tra entrambi i contendenti, esisteva un'ampia frangia di terreno denominata "terra di nessuno", in cui si succedette un'infinità di avanzate e ritirate, al prezzo di innumerevoli vittime. Il primo giorno dell'assalto alle linee tedesche, il 1 luglio, sarà ricordato da solo come il più tragico della storia dell'esercito del Regno Unito, in cui morirono quasi 20.000 soldati britannici. Le scarse difese delle truppe contro il nemico, nella fangosa terra di nessuno, portò alla precipitosa introduzione di una nuova arma da combattimento, il carro armato, che si utilizzò per la prima volta nel Somme. Questa terribile battaglia fu immortalata per i posteri nel primo documentario bellico della storia.

ケシの花が埋め尽くす美しい平原の下で、何十年も前、地獄のような塹壕戦の象徴ともなった世界大戦の中でも最も多くの血が流れた戦いが行われたとは誰もが予想しないでしょう。1916年、フランスのヴェルダン要塞に対するドイツ軍の攻撃は日増しに激しくなってきました。そこで連合国側のイギリス軍が、フランスとベルギーの国境にいる敵国ドイツの戦線を攻撃して、ヴェルダンから注意をそらせようとしました。しかし、その結果は惨憺たるものでした。6ヶ月の激しい戦闘の結果、百万人以上の犠牲者（うち300,000人が死亡）を出し、たった8キロ前進しただけでした。

連合国軍も同盟国軍も、その当時ヨーロッパに多く存在した「どちらにも属さない」土地で、数知れない戦いを繰り広げ、それに合わせて無数の負傷者と死者を出しました。ドイツ軍の塹壕への攻撃開始の日に、20,000人ものイギリス人兵士が犠牲となり、イギリス軍の歴史の中でも悲劇の日として記憶されるようになりました。このソンムの戦いで、「誰のものでもない」泥まみれの土地でドイツ軍を攻撃するため、その当時としては画期的な兵器であった戦車がイギリス軍によって投入されました。この激しい戦いは、数ある戦いの中でも記録に残る悲惨な戦闘としてその後も語り継がれています。

fra   ℹ   Article Wikipèdia

ita   ℹ   Articolo Wikipedia

jap   ℹ   ウィキペディアの記事

Battle of the Somme

1916 The Battle of Somme
Central Europe – World War I

Bajo un suave manto de amapolas se ocultan hoy los restos de una de las más sangrientas batallas de la Gran Guerra, convertida en icono de la infernal lucha de trincheras. En 1916 la presión alemana sobre los franceses en la zona de Verdún se hacía cada vez más intensa. El alto mando británico decide entonces realizar un movimiento de distracción rompiendo las líneas enemigas en la frontera franco-belga. Las consecuencias fueron devastadoras; tras seis meses de duros combates y más de un millón de bajas (de ellas 300.000 muertos) sólo se consiguió avanzar 8 km.

Entre ambos contendientes existía una amplia franja de terreno denominada "tierra de nadie" donde se sucedieron un sinfín de avances y retrocesos a costa de innumerables bajas. Tan sólo el primer día de asalto a las líneas alemanas, el 1 de julio, será recordado como el más trágico de la historia del ejército del Reino Unido, en el que murieron casi 20.000 soldados británicos. La indefensión de las tropas ante el enemigo en la fangosa tierra de nadie llevó a la precipitada introducción de una nueva arma de combate, el carro de combate, que se utilizó por primera vez en el Somme. Esta terrible batalla quedó reflejada para la posteridad en el primer documental bélico de la Historia.

Under a soft shawl of poppies, the remains of one of the bloodiest Great War battles are nowadays hidden. The have become a symbol of the terrible trench fighting. In 1916 the German pressure on the French people at Verdun was increasingly intense. The British high command then decides to carry out a distraction movement, breaking the enemy lines at the French-Belgian frontier. Consequences were devastating, after six months of hard fighting and more than a million of casualties (300,000 dead people among them) it was possible to advance only 8 kilometres.

There was a wide strip of land between both enemies, it was called "nobody's land". There were uncountable advances and backward movements, costing innumerable lives. The first day of the assault to German troops, on July 1st, shall be remembered as the most tragic in the United Kingdom's history, because almost 20,000 British soldiers died in that moment. As the troops were defenceless in the presence of the enemy, at the muddy nobody's land, a new fighting weapon hastily introduced, the combat car, which was firstly used at the Somme. This terrible battle was immortalized for future generations in the first war documentary of the History.

Unter einer weichen Decke Mohnblumen sind heute die Reste einer der blutigsten Schlachten des Ersten Weltkrieges versteckt, die zur Ikone der infernalischen Grabenkämpfe geworden ist. 1916 wurde der deutsche Druck auf die Franzosen in der Gegend um Verdun immer größer. Die britischen Anführer entscheiden sich für ein Ablenkungsmanöver und durchbrechen die feindlichen Linien an der französisch-belgischen Front. Die Folgen waren verheerend: nach sechs Monaten hartem Kampf und mehr als einer Million Opfer (300.000 Tote) war man nur 8 km vorangekommen.

Zwischen den beiden kämpfenden Seiten gab es einen breiten Abschnitt, der „Niemandsland" genannt wurde und auf dem unzählige Vorstöße und Rückzüge vorgenommen wurden, die viele Opfer forderten. Allein der erste Tag des Angriffs auf die deutschen Linien am 1. Juli ging in die Geschichte ein als der tragischste Tag des britischen Heers, an dem fast 20.000 britische Soldaten fielen. Die Truppen waren in dem Morast des Niemandslands dem Feind schutzlos ausgeliefert, was zu der überstürzten Einführung einer neuen Waffe, dem Panzer führte, der zum ersten Mal in der Schlacht an der Somme eingesetzt wurde. Diese entsetzliche Schlacht wurde für die Nachwelt im ersten Kriegsdokumentarfilm der Geschichte festgehalten.

esp ⓘ Artículo Wikipedia

eng ⓘ Wikipedia Article

deu ⓘ Wikipedia-Artikel

THE BATTLE OF SOMME

1916

Gallipoli

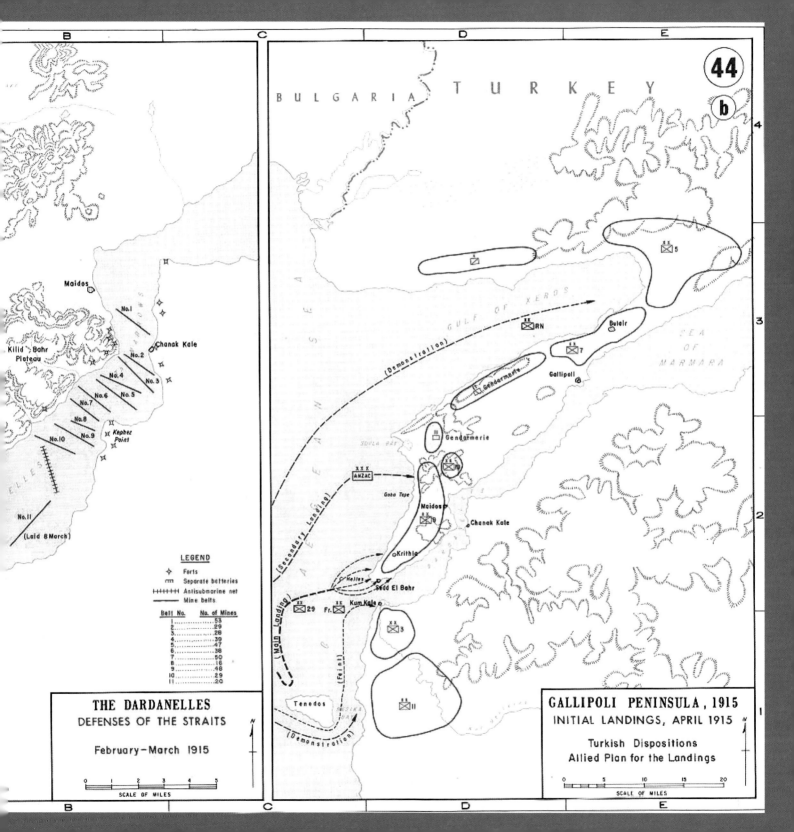

44

b

BULGARIA   TURKEY

AEGEAN SEA

GULF OF XEROS

SEA OF MARMARA

(Demonstration)

XX RN

XX 5

Bulair

XX 7

Gallipoli

II Gendarmerie

II Gendarmerie

SUVLA BAY

XXX ANZAC

XX 19

Gaba Tepe

XX 9

Maidos

Chanak Kale

Krithia

Helles

Sedd El Bahr

(Secondary Landing)

(Main Landing)

(Feint)

XX 29

Fr. XX

Kum Kale

XX 3

Tenedos

(Demonstration)

XX 11

GALLIPOLI PENINSULA, 1915
INITIAL LANDINGS, APRIL 1915

Turkish Dispositions
Allied Plan for the Landings

0   5   10   15   20
SCALE OF MILES

N

Maidos

No.1

Chanak Kale

Kilid Bahr Plateau

No.2

No.4

No.3

No.6

No.5

No.7

No.8

No.9

Kephez Point

No.10

THE NARROWS

HELLES

No.11

(Laid 8 March)

LEGEND

✧ Forts
⌐⌐ Separate batteries
┼┼┼┼┼ Antisubmarine net
—— Mine belts

Belt No.	No. of Mines
1	53
2	29
3	28
4	39
5	47
6	38
7	50
8	16
9	48
10	29
11	20

THE DARDANELLES
DEFENSES OF THE STRAITS

February–March 1915

N

0   1   2   3   4   5
SCALE OF MILES

GULF OF XEROS

SUVLA BAY

4

3

Krithia

2

Tekke Burnu

C. Helles   Şedd El Bahr

Kum Kale

1

BESIKA BAY

A

ROYAL NAVY
BATTLESHIPS

Frank Clarck's Letter

Gallipoli 1915

© Illustration par Carrey pour le journal *Le Miroir*. 1915

Seulement un an après le début de la Ire Guerre mondiale, se produit le plus affreux carnage perpétré au cours d'une guerre, qui changera à tout jamais l'Humanité. Les forces anglo-françaises décident d'entreprendre une opération risquée et combinée en débarquant dans la péninsule de Gallipoli, en Turquie, alliée de l'Allemagne. Elles visaient le contrôle du stratégique détroit des Dardanelles et voulaient ainsi permettre la connexion avec la Russie et faire pression par l'arrière-garde sur les puissances centrales. La bataille a duré presque un an et le tribut payé fut lourd : près d'un million de victimes pour les deux armées. Elle s'est également soldée par la victoire turque.

Les forces de l'ANZAC (Corps de l'armée australienne et néozélandaise) ont joué un rôle important. Courageuse, elles ont payé en vies humaines et ont scellé les relations entre les deux pays. Pour la Turquie, cela a supposé la confirmation comme entité nationale, ce qui, après la défaite et la dissolution de l'Empire ottoman à la fin de la Grande Guerre, a donné lieu à une sanglante lutte d'indépendance menée par Moustapha Kemal, général en chef des forces turques pendant la bataille de Gallipoli. Aujourd'hui encore, les empreintes de la bataille sont visibles sur toute la péninsule.

Solo un anno dopo l'inizio della I Guerra Mondiale, si produsse una delle prime carneficine di una guerra che cambierà l'umanità. Le forze anglo-francesi decisero di intraprendere una rischiosa operazione combinata sbarcando nella Penisola di Gallipoli, in Turchia, alleata della Germania. Con questa azione si puntava al controllo dello strategico Stretto dei Dardanelli, per permettere così la connessione con la Russia e mettere pressione alle potenze centrali dalla loro retroguardia. La battaglia durò quasi un anno, col terribile bilancio di quasi mezzo milione di vittime tra i due eserciti e con la finale vittoria turca.

Un ruolo di rilievo fu quello delle forze dell'ANZAC (Corpo dell'Esercito Australiano e Neozelandese), il cui coraggio e tributo in vite umane sigillarono le relazioni tra entrambi i paesi. Per la Turchia questa battaglia costituì la sua conferma come entità nazionale, cosa che, dopo la sconfitta e la dissoluzione dell'Impero Ottomano alla fine della Grande Guerra, diede luogo al cruento processo di indipendenza sotto la guida di Mustafà Kemal, generale in capo delle forze turche durante la battaglia di Gallipoli. Ancora oggi, nella vasta penisola, si possono ritrovare le tracce della battaglia.

人類史を変えることになる第一次世界大戦が始まって1年しか経たないうちに、その戦争の中でも最初の激しい戦いのうちのひとつが起こりました。イギリス、フランス連合軍は、その当時ドイツと同盟していたトルコのガリポリ半島（現在のゲリボル）に危険を冒しての上陸作戦を決行することにしました。その目的は、ダーダネルス海峡を支配下に置き、ロシアとの連携を容易にし、また、中央ヨーロッパ諸国も連合国側に入れるためでした。この戦いは1年ほど続き、その結果はトルコの勝利でしたが、トルコ軍と連合軍が出した犠牲者はおよそ50万人を超えると言われています。

オーストラリア・ニュージーランド軍団（通称ANZAC）は、この戦いで、その勇敢さと敵の兵士の「命」をも大切にする寛大な精神を持つことで世界に知られるようになりました。また、トルコにとっては、この戦いは国民の意識を高揚させ、オスマン帝国の解体とその後のムスタファ・ケマル（またはケマル・パシャ）をリーダーとした祖国解放運動に拍車をかけることになりました。このムスタファ・ケマルは、ガリポリ戦争で活躍したトルコ軍人の一人です。そして今日でも、この戦いの傷跡はガリポリ半島のいたるところに見られます。

fra ⓘ Article Wikipèdia

ita ⓘ Articolo Wikipedia

jap ⓘ ウィキペディアの記事

Gallipoli Battlefield

1915 Gallipoli
Central Europe – World War I

○

Tan sólo un año después del comienzo de la I Guerra Mundial se produce una de las primeras sangrías humanas de una guerra que cambiará a la Humanidad. Las fuerzas anglo-francesas deciden emprender una arriesgada operación combinada desembarcando en la Península de Gallipoli en Turquía, aliada de Alemania. Con ello se buscaba el control del estratégico estrecho de los Dardanelos y permitir así la conexión con Rusia y presionar por la retaguardia a las potencias centrales. La batalla duró casi un año con el terrible saldo de casi medio millón de víctimas entre los dos ejércitos y la victoria turca.

Papel destacado lo tuvieron las fuerzas del ANZAC (Cuerpo de Ejército Australiano-Neozelandés) cuya valerosidad y tributo en vidas sellaron las relaciones entre ambos países. Para Turquía supuso la confirmación como entidad nacional lo que, tras la derrota y disolución del Imperio Otomano al finalizar la Gran Guerra, dio lugar a un cruento proceso de independencia liderado por Mustafá Kemal, general en jefe de las fuerzas turcas durante la batalla de Gallipoli. Todavía hoy son perceptibles las huellas de la batalla en la extensa península.

✹

Only a year after the beginning of the World War I, one of the first human bleedings which shall change Mankind, took place. British and French forces decide to start a risky combined operation, disembarking in Gallipoli Peninsula in Turkey, allied with Germany. The purpose was to gain strategic control of the Dardanelles, allowing thus the connection with Russia, putting pressure on central powers by the rearguard. The battle lasted almost a year with the terrible result of about half million casualties between both armies and the Turkish victory.

The ANZAC forces (Australian and New Zealand Army Corps) had an outstanding role, and their braveness and the lives they offered, strengthened links between both nations. For Turkey it meant its confirmation as national entity, which, after the defeat and dissolution of the Ottoman Empire at the end of the Great War, gave origin to a cruel independence process led by Mustafa Kemal, chief general of the Turkish forces during the battle of Gallipoli. Even nowadays, it is possible to perceive the marks of the battle in the wide peninsula.

○

Nur ein Jahr nach Ausbruch des Ersten Weltkriegs wird eine der blutigsten Schlachten der Geschichte in einem Krieg geschlagen, der die Welt verändern sollte. Die englisch-französischen Truppen beschließen eine riskante gemeinsame Operation, bei der Sie auf der Halbinsel Gallipoli in der Türkei landen, die mit Deutschland alliiert war. Hiermit wollte man die Kontrolle über die strategische Meerenge der Dardanellen erreichen und so die Verbindung mit Russland herstellen, sowie den Nachtrupp der Zentralen Mächte unter Druck setzen. Die Schlacht dauerte fast ein Jahr mit dem entsetzlichen Ergebnis von fast einer halben Million Opfern auf beiden Seiten und dem Sieg der Türkei.

Die ANZAC-Truppen (Australian and Newzealand Army Corps) spielten eine entscheidende Rolle und durch ihre Tapferkeit und Opfer wurde die Beziehungen zwischen beiden Ländern besiegelt. Für die Türkei bedeutete dies die Bestätigung als nationale Entität, aus der sich nach der Zerschlagung des Ottomanischen Reichs nach dem Ende des Ersten Weltkriegs der grausame Unabhängigkeitsprozess unter Mustafa Kema entwickelte, der General des türkischen Heers in der Schlacht von Gallipoli. Noch heute sind die Spuren der Schlacht auf der Halbinsel sichtbar.

esp ⓘ Artículo Wikipedia

eng ⓘ Wikipedia Article

deu ⓘ Wikipedia-Artikel

GALLIPOLI

1915

Cetshwayo kaMpande

Zulu kids dancing

Zulu Dawn 1/3

La Guerre Anglo-Zouloue doit s'inscrire dans le processus d'expansion coloniale britannique en Afrique du Sud, un territoire riche en diamants et en or, qui a affronté la Grande Bretagne et le peuple zoulou et ensuite avec les colons hollandais pendant les Guerres des Boers.

En 1878, le roi Zoulou Cetshwayo s'oppose à une série de mesures de pression axées à miner son pouvoir et les Britanniques en profitent pour poser un ultimatum. Avant que le roi ne puisse ne serait-ce qu'y répondre, l'armée britannique déclare la guerre (1879) et entre dans le territoire zoulou. Le corps expéditionnaire, dirigé par le Baron de Chelmsford, était composé par plusieurs régiments de cavalerie, d'infanterie et de volontaires qui totalisaient environ 17 000 hommes. Par excès de confiance, les troupes campent à Isandhlwana, une zone ouverte et sans aucun type de protection. Alors que Chelmsford sort à la recherche de l'ennemi, 35 régiments zoulous (22 000 guerriers) complètement cachés et commandés par le chef Ntshingwayo Khoza attaquent par surprise et anéantissent la garnison de l'arrière-garde (1 800 hommes).

Ce fut la première défaite britannique dans une guerre meurtrière qui a fini avec l'occupation de la capitale zouloue d'Ulundi et l'exile de son roi. Curieusement, Cetshwayo a été remis à son trône trois ans après par ses propres vainqueurs.

La Guerra Anglo-Zulù si inserisce nel processo dell'espansione coloniale britannica in Sudafrica, un paese ricco d'oro e di diamanti, che contrappose la Gran Bretagna alla popolazione indigena Zulù e in seguito ai coloni olandesi, nella Guerra dei Boeri.

Nel 1878 il re Zulù Cetshwayo si oppose ad una serie di misure di pressione volte a minare il suo potere e che gli inglesi sfruttano per lanciargli un ultimatum. Prima che il re potesse anche solo rispondere, l'esercito britannico dichiarò la guerra (1879) ed entrò in territorio zulù. Il corpo di spedizione diretto dal Barone di Chelmsford era composto da vari reggimenti di cavalleria, fanteria e volontari, per un totale di circa 17.000 uomini. In un eccesso di fiducia, le truppe si accamparono ad Isandhlwana, in una zona aperta e senza nessun tipo di protezione. Mentre Chelmsford andava a caccia del nemico, 35 reggimenti zulù (circa 22.000 combattenti), totalmente nascosti e diretti dal capo Ntshingwayo Khoza, attaccarono a sorpresa ed annientarono la guarnigione della retroguardia (1.800 uomini).

Si trattò della prima sconfitta britannica in una cruenta guerra che terminò con l'occupazione della capitale zulù di Ulundi e l'esilio del suo re. Curiosamente Cetshwayo fu riposto sul trono tre anni più tardi dai suoi stessi vincitori.

イギリス帝国とズールー族の戦いは、南アフリカにおけるヨーロッパ列強国の殖民地拡大の過程において、ひとつの区切りとなりました。この戦い以降も、ダイアモンドや金の豊富な南アフリカは、オランダ系移民の子孫たちであるボーア人がこの地方を手に入れようとしますが、イギリス帝国はこれらの財宝を狙ってズール族と激しい戦いをすることになりました。

1878年、ズールー族の王セツワヨは、イギリス帝国がその勢力を弱めようと、この部族に対してあらゆる手段を使ってくるのに抵抗していました。しかし、1879年、セツワヨがイギリスの最後通牒に返事する前に、イギリス軍は宣戦布告をし、ズールー族の土地へ侵入しました。チェルムスフォード男爵に率いられた遠征軍は、騎兵隊、歩兵隊、志願兵を含め17,000人の兵士から成る部隊でした。そして、彼らは自分たちの勝利を過信し、イサンドゥルワナの隠れるとこや非難できる場所のない平野に駐屯しました。チェルムスフォード男爵がズールー族を探しに行っている間に、密かに隠れていた35連隊22,000人のズールー族兵士たちが油断していたイギリス軍の駐屯兵士たち1,800人に奇襲をかけました。

このイギリス帝国軍の最初の敗北は、結果としてズールー王国の首都占領の終了となりました。また、その王であるセツワヨはロンドンに留置されていましたが、南アフリカの部族間の抗争鎮圧のため、この戦いの3年後、イギリス帝国によって再び王位に戻されました。

fra ⓘ Article Wikipèdia

ita ⓘ Articolo Wikipedia

jap ⓘ ウィキペディアの記事

flick © Richard Gifford

Zulu Battlefield

1879 Isandhlwana
Southafrica – Anglo-Zulu War

La Guerra Anglo-Zulú debe enmarcarse en el proceso de expansión colonial británico en Sudáfrica, rica en diamantes y oro, que enfrentó a Gran Bretaña con el pueblo nativo Zulú y posteriormente con los colonos holandeses en las Guerras de los Bóers.

En 1878 el rey Zulú Cetshwayo se opone a una serie de medidas de presión encaminadas a socavar su poder lo que aprovechan los británicos para lanzar un ultimátum. Antes de que el rey pudiese siquiera responder, el ejército británico declara la guerra (1879) y entra en territorio Zulú. El cuerpo expedicionario, dirigido por el Barón de Chelmsford, estaba compuesto por varios regimientos de caballería, infantería y voluntarios que totalizaban unos 17.000 hombres. En un exceso de confianza las tropas acampan en Isandhlwana, una zona abierta y sin ningún tipo de protección. Mientras Chelmsford sale en busca del enemigo, 35 regimientos zulúes (22.000 guerreros) completamente ocultos y dirigidos por el jefe Ntshingwayo Khoza atacan por sorpresa y aniquilan a la guarnición de retaguardia (1.800 hombres).

Fue la primera derrota británica en una sangrienta guerra que acabó con la ocupación de la capital Zulú de Ulundi y el destierro de su rey. Curiosamente Cetshwayo fue repuesto en su trono tres años después por sus propios vencedores.

Anglo-Zulu war must be understood within the British colonial expansion process in South Africa, rich in diamonds and gold. This process set at odds Great Britain with the native Zulu people and afterwards with the Dutch settler, during the Boers war.

In 1878 the Zulu king Cetshwayo showed his opposition to measures tending to undermine his power; this opposition was used by Great Britain to issue an ultimatum. Before the king could even respond, the British army declared war (1879) and entered Zulu territory. The expeditionary group, led by Baron Chelmsford, was comprised of several cavalry and infantry regiments, along with volunteers, forming a total of about 17,000 men. Being extremely self-confident, the troops camp at an open area, Isandhlwana, without any kind of protection. While Chelmsford seeks the enemy, 35 zulu regiments (22,000 warriors) completely hidden and led by chief Ntshingwayo Khoza attack by surprise and kill the rearguard troop (1,800).

It was the first British defeat in a bloody war which ended with the occupation of the Zulu capital, Ulundi, and their king's exile. Curiously, Cetshwayo was put back in his throne three years later, by his own winners.

Der Krieg zwischen dem britischen Empire und der Zulu-Nation muss im Rahmen der kolonialen Ausbreitung Großbritanniens in Südafrika gesehen werden, ein Land, das reich an Diamanten und Gold ist. Großbritannien sah sich dem Eingeborenenvolk der Zulus gegenüber und anschließend den holländischen Siedlern in den Boerskriegen.

1878 widersetzt sich der Zulukönig Cetshwayo einer Reihe von Maßnahmen, die darauf abzielten, seine Macht zu unterdrücken, was von den Briten genutzt wurde, um ein Ultimatum zu setzen. Bevor der König überhaupt antworten konnte, erklärte das britische Heer den Krieg (1879) und dringt in Zulu-Gebiet ein. Die vom Baron von Chelmsford geführten Truppen bestanden aus mehreren Regimenten Kavallerie, Infanterie und Freiwilligen, die insgesamt etwa 17.000 Männer umfassten. Sich in Sicherheit wiegend kampierten die Truppen in Isandhlwana, einem offenen Gebiet ohne Schutz. Während Chelmsford auszieht, den Feind zu finden, greifen 35 Zuluregimenter (22.000 Krieger) aus dem Versteck unter Leitung des Häuptlings Ntshingwayo Khoza überraschend an und löschen den Nachtrupp aus (1.800 Männer).

Dies war die erste britische Niederlage in einem blutigen Krieg, der mit der Besetzung der Zuluhauptstadt Ulundi und der Verbannung des Königs endete. Erstaunlicherweise wurde Cetshwayo drei Jahre später von den Siegern selbst wieder auf den Thron gebracht.

esp ⓘ Artículo Wikipedia

eng ⓘ Wikipedia Article

deu ⓘ Wikipedia-Artikel

1879

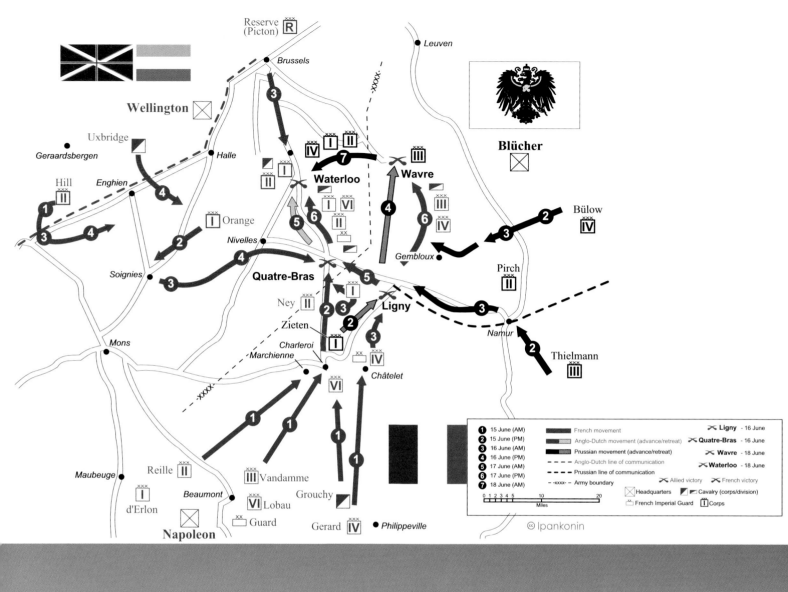

Reserve
(Picton) R

Wellington ⊠

Uxbridge

Geraardsbergen

Hill III

Enghien

Orange I

Nivelles

Soignies

Quatre-Bras

Ney II

Zieten

Charleroi

Marchienne

Mons

Châtelet

Reille II

Maubeuge

Beaumont

d'Erlon I

III Vandamme

VI Lobau

Guard

Napoleon

Gerard IV

Philippeville

Grouchy

Brussels

Halle

IV I II

Waterloo

I VI

II

Wavre

III

Gembloux

Blücher ⊠

Pirch II

Namur

Bülow IV

Leuven

		15 June (AM)		French movement		⚔ **Ligny** - 16 June
	❷	15 June (PM)		Anglo-Dutch movement (advance/retreat)		⚔ **Quatre-Bras** - 16 June
	❸	16 June (AM)		Prussian movement (advance/retreat)		⚔ **Wavre** - 18 June
	❹	16 June (PM)		Anglo-Dutch line of communication		⚔ **Waterloo** - 18 June
	❺	17 June (AM)		Prussian line of communication		
	❻	17 June (PM)		Army boundary		
	❼	18 June (AM)				⚔ Allied victory ⚔ French victory

Headquarters ⊠   Cavalry (corps/division)

French Imperial Guard   Corps I

0 1 2 3 4 5   10   20
Miles

© Ipankonin

Hougoumont

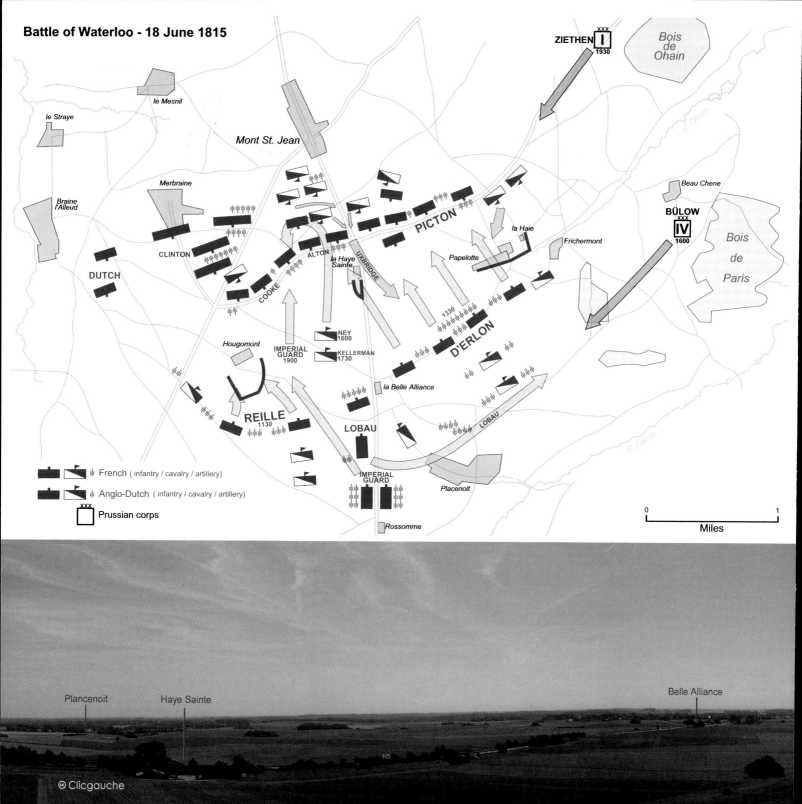

Battle of Waterloo - 18 June 1815

Bois de Ohain

ZIETHEN | I | 1930

le Straye

le Mesnil

Mont St. Jean

Braine l'Alleud

Merbraine

Beau Chene

BÜLOW | IV | 1600

Bois de Paris

CLINTON

DUTCH

COOKE

ALTON

la Haye Sainte

UXBRIDGE

PICTON

la Haie

Papelotte

Frichermont

1330

D'ERLON

Hougomont

IMPERIAL GUARD 1900

NEY 1600

KELLERMAN 1730

la Belle Alliance

REILLE 1130

LOBAU

LOBAU

R. Lasne

IMPERIAL GUARD

Placenoit

Rossomme

French (infantry / cavalry / artillery)

Anglo-Dutch (infantry / cavalry / artillery)

xxx Prussian corps

0   1

Miles

Plancenoit   Haye Sainte

Belle Alliance

N5

© Clicgauche

Sir Arthur Wellesley, 1st Duke of Wellington
by Francisco de Goya

Battle 2007

The Horse Grenadiers. Waterloo

La bataille de Waterloo. 18 juin 1815
by Clément-Auguste Andrieux

Waterloo

À seulement 20 km de Bruxelles, entre de douces pentes et de vertes prairies, s'est livrée à la mi-juin 1815 une des plus sanglantes batailles des « Guerres napoléoniennes ». Après son exil sur l'île d'Elbe, Napoléon décide de récupérer la Couronne impériale avec l'aide du peuple français et de ses anciens commandants. Avant que les puissances rivales de l'Europe ne puissent se forger une union solide pour soumettre de nouveau la France, Napoléon réagit et envahit les Pays-Bas.

Les forces de la « Septième Coalition », commandées par le duc de Wellington, étaient formées par les armées de Prusse, du Royaume-Uni et de la Hollande et comptaient avec environ 230 000 hommes et plus de 500 canons. Les troupes et l'artillerie allemandes du maréchal Von Blücher comprenaient plus de 50 % du total allié et ce sont eux qui ont apporté la plus grande part à la bataille. Du côté français, les célèbres maréchaux Ney et De Grouchy commandaient environ 123 000 hommes et possédaient 366 canons. Malgré l'infériorité numérique évidente de l'armée française, Napoléon a essayé par tous les moyens de diviser les armées alliées et de les vaincre les unes après les autres. Toutefois, la farouche détermination prussienne à combattre en combinaison avec les troupes britanniques et l'audace finale de celles-ci ont contribué à la victoire. Napoléon ne combattra jamais plus.

A soli 20 km da Bruxelles, tra dolci pendii e prati verdi, ebbe luogo a metà di giugno del 1815 una delle battaglie più cruente delle cosiddette "Guerre Napoleoniche". Dopo essere fuggito sull'Isola d'Elba, Napoleone decise di recuperare la Corona Imperiale con l'appoggio del popolo francese e dei suoi vecchi comandanti. Prima che si potesse forgiare una solida unione tra le potenze rivali in Europa per sottomettere nuovamente la Francia, Napoleone reagì invadendo i Paesi Bassi.

Le forze della "Settima Coalizione", dirette dal duca di Wellington, erano formate dagli eserciti di Prusia, Regno Unito e Olanda con circa 230.000 uomini e più di 500 cannoni. Le truppe e l'artiglieria del maresciallo von Blücher comprendevano più del del 50% del totale delle forze alleate e furono loro in effetti a sopportare il grosso della battaglia. Dalla parte francese, i famosi marescialli Ney e De Grouchy comandavano circa 123.000 uomini con 366 cannoni. Nonostante l'esercito francese si trovasse in un'evidente inferiorità numerica, Napoleone cercò in tutti i modi di separare gli eserciti alleati e di sconfiggerli uno per uno, ma la ferrea determinazione prussiana di combattere insieme alle truppe britanniche e l'audacia finale di queste ultime contribuirono alla vittoria. Napoleone non avrebbe combattuto mai più.

ブリュッセルからわずか20キロ、なだらかな起伏のある牧草地が広がる一見穏やかな風景ですが、この場所で1815年の6月に、有名な「ナポレオン戦争」の中でも最も激しい戦いが繰り広げられました。ナポレオンは、エルバ島を脱出した後、皇帝の地位を取り戻そうと、フランス国民と軍隊の仲間の協力を得ました。そして、ヨーロッパの列強が共同してその威力を高め、フランスを攻撃する前に、ナポレオンはまずオランダを攻めました。

ウェリントン公に率いられた第7次対仏大同盟は、プロイセン、イギリス、オランダから構成され、兵士の数は230,000人、大砲は500砲という大軍でした。陸軍元帥ビュルッヘルのドイツ軍とその砲兵隊は同盟諸国軍の半数の兵士を所有し、ワーテルローの戦いに参加しました。一方、フランス軍のほうは、ネイ元帥やド・グリューシー元帥に率いられた123,000人の兵士と366門の大砲がありました。ナポレオン軍は、数の上では対仏同盟軍に劣っていましたが、それらの各国の軍隊をばらばらにして、各々を壊滅するという方法を取りました。しかし、プロイセン軍は、イギリス軍と共に戦うという姿勢を一貫して保ち、またその大胆不敵な行動でとうとうフランス軍を負かして勝利を勝ち取りました。ナポレオンは、この戦いを最後にしてその短くも華麗な戦史を閉じることになりました。

fra ⓘ Article Wikipèdia

ita ⓘ Articolo Wikipedia

jap ⓘ ウィキペディアの記事

Napoleon Crossing the Alps
by Jacques-Louis David

Waterloo 1815

1815 Waterloo
Central Europe – Napoleonic Wars

A tan sólo 20 km de Bruselas, entre suaves pendientes y verdes prados, se desarrolló a mediados de junio de 1815 una de las más cruentas batallas de las conocidas como "Guerras Napoleónicas". Tras su huida del exilio en la Isla de Elba, Napoleón decide recuperar la Corona Imperial con el apoyo del pueblo francés y de sus antiguos comandantes. Antes de que pudiese forjarse una sólida unión entre las potencias rivales de Europa para someter de nuevo a Francia, Napoleón reacciona e invade los Países Bajos.

Las fuerzas de la "Séptima Coalición", dirigidas por el duque de Wellington, estaban formadas por los ejércitos de Prusia, Reino Unido y Holanda con unos 230.000 hombres y más de 500 cañones. Las tropas y artillería alemanas del mariscal von Blücher comprendían más del 50% del total aliado y fueron quienes llevaron el grueso de la batalla. Por parte francesa los renombrados mariscales Ney y De Grouchy comandaban a unos 123.000 hombres y 366 cañones. Aunque el ejército francés contaba con una clara inferioridad numérica, Napoleón trató por todos los medios de separar a los ejércitos aliados y derrotarlos uno a uno, pero la férrea determinación prusiana de combatir en combinación con las tropas británicas y la audacia final de estas contribuyó a la victoria. Napoleón no volvería a combatir jamás.

In the middle of June, 1815, at only 20 km from Brussels, between soft slopes and green fields, one of the most bloody battles among those known as "Napoleonic Wars" took place. After escaping from exile at Elba Island, Napoleon decides to recover the Imperial Crown, supported by the French people and his old commanding officers. Before a solid union among rival powerful countries could emerge so as to subdue France again, Napoleon reacts and invades the Netherlands.

"The Seventh Coalition" forces, led by the Duke of Wellington, were comprised of armies from Prussia, the United Kingdom and Holland with about 230,000 men and more than 500 cannons. Marshal von Blücher's German troops and artillery encompassed more than 50% of the allies, and they were the ones who carried out the most important part of the battle. On the French side, the well known marshals Ney and De Grouchy commanded about 123,000 men and 366 cannons. Although the French army was clearly numerically inferior, Napoleon tried by all means to split the allied troops and to defeat them one by one; but the Prussian iron determination to fight together with British troops and their final audacity, contributed to victory. Napoleon was not going to fight any longer.

Nur 20 km vor Brüssel entfernt spielte sich Mitte Juni 1815 zwischen sanften Hügeln und grünen Feldern eine der grausamsten Schlachten der so genannten „Napoleonischen Kriege" ab. Nachdem Napoleon aus dem Exil auf der Insel Elba geflohen war, beschloss er, die Kaiserkrone mit der Unterstützung des französischen Volkes und der alten Kommandanten zurückzuerobern. Napoleon reagiert und besetzt die Niederlande, noch bevor sich zwischen den feindlichen Mächten Europas eine solide Verbindung bilden konnte.

Die Mächte der „Siebten Koalition", die vom Duque of Wellington angeführt wurden, bestanden aus dem preußischen, englischen und niederländischen Heer mit etwa 230.000 Männern und über 500 Kanonen. Die deutschen Truppen und Artillerie des Marschalls von Blücher machten mehr als 50% der gesamten Alliierten aus und übernahmen den Großteil der Schlacht. Auf französischer Seiten führten Marschal Ney und De Grouchy etwa 123.000 Männer und 366 Kanonen in die Schlacht. Obwohl das französische Heer anzahlmäßig stark unterlegen war, versuchte Napoleon mit allen Mitteln die alliierten Heere zu trennen und einzeln zu besiegen. Aber die eiserne preußische Entschlossenheit, zusammen mit den britischen Truppen zu kämpfen und das finale Wagnis derselben trugen zum Sieg bei. Napoleon sollte nie wieder kämpfen.

esp ⓘ Artículo Wikipedia

eng ⓘ Wikipedia Article

deu ⓘ Wikipedia-Artikel

1815

Es · Instale el Kaywa Reader en su móvil accediendo desde su ordenador o teléfono a http://reader.kaywa.com

En · Install Kaywa Reader in your mobile phone by clicking http://reader.kaywa.com through your PC or phone.

De · Installiere den Kaywa Reader auf deinem Handy, indem du von deinem Computer oder Telefon aus auf http://reader.kaywa.com gehst.

Fr · Installer le Kaywa Reader dans votre portable en accédant depuis votre ordinateur ou téléphone à la page suivante http://reader.kaywa.com

It · Installate Kaywa Reader nel vostro cellulare collegandovi via pc o cellulare a http://reader.kaywa.com

Ja · パソコンか携帯電話を使用して、お使いの携帯電話へKaywa Readerをインストールしましょう。http://reader.kaywa.com

Es · Abra el Kaywa Reader y enfoque al QR y le aparecerá el contenido del código.

En · Open Kaywa Reader and zoom in QR; the code content will pop up.

De · Öffne den Kaywa Reader und fokussiere auf den QR, damit du den Inhalt des Codes sehen kannst.

Fr · Ouvrir le Kaywa Reader et pointer vers le QR et le contenu du code apparaîtra.

It · Aprite Kaywa Reader e portate il cursore su QR: vi apparirà il contenuto del codice.

Ja · Kaywa Readerを開いてQRコードにカメラをあてて読み取ると、コードが解読されます。

Es · Al aceptar, se abrirá otra ventana con el contenido del QR.

En · When accepting, another window with the QR content will pop up.

De · Sobald du auf OK drückst, öffnet sich ein neues Fenster mit dem Inhalt des QR.

Fr · Après avoir accepté, une autre fenêtre s'ouvrira avec le contenu du QR.

It · Selezionando "Accetta", si aprirà un'altra finestra con il contenuto del QR.

Ja · 読み取れると、QRコードに含まれたデータの詳細を表すウィンドウが開きます。

Que sont les codes QR?

Les codes QR (Quick Response Codes) sont des codes-barres en 2 dimensions. Pour lire leur contenu, un lecteur spécial est nécessaire. Par rapport aux codes traditionnels, les QR peuvent stocker beaucoup plus d'information en forme de texte ou de liens à des sites web.

Qui les utilise?

Lancés en 2004, ces codes sont massivement utilisés au Japon. Récemment, avec les appareils photo des téléphones portables, ils sont de plus en plus employés en Europe et Amérique.

Qu'est-ce que le Kaywa Reader?

Le Kaywa Reader est une application pour portables qui permet de lire les codes QR en utilisant l'appareil photo du téléphone portable. Dans certains cas, les fabricants de téléphones incorporent déjà une application pour lire ces codes, comme c'est le cas du Nokia N95.

Quels téléphones sont compatibles?

http://reader.kaywa.com/phones

Motorola E770, RAZR V3x.

Nokia 3230, 3250, 5300, 6136, 6233, 6260, 6270, 6280, 6288, 6600, 6620, 6630, 6670, 6680, 6681, 6682, 7610, E65, N70, N71, N73, N80, N90, N91, N93, N95.

Samsung SGH-Z500.

SonyEricsson K300i, K510i, K700i, K750i, K800i, S710a, V630, V800, W300i, W550i, W710i, W800i, W810i, W850i, Z520a, Z520i, Z610i.

Est-ce gratuit?

Oui, l'application pour lire les codes est gratuite. Toutefois, pour accéder aux contenus, il faut pouvoir accéder à Internet à travers le portable. Veuillez consulter les tarifs avec votre opérateur. Il est conseillé d'avoir un forfait de données ou utiliser une connexion Wifi.

Cosa sono i codici QR?

I codici QR (Quick Response Codes) sono dei codici a barre bidimensionali. Per leggerne il contenuto è necessario un lettore speciale. Rispetto ai codici tradizionali, i QR possono immagazzinare molte informazioni in forma di testo o di URL.

Chi li utilizza?

A partire dal 2004, il Giappone è il paese che maggiormente usa abitualmente questi codici. Di recente, con le nuove videocamere dei cellulari, il suo uso si sta estendendo in Europa e in America.

Cos'è il Kaywa Reader?

Kaywa Reader è un'applicazione per cellulari che permette di leggere i codici QR tramite la videocamera del telefonino. In alcuni casi i fabbricanti di telefonini integrano in partenza delle applicazioni per leggere questi codici, come nel caso del Nokia N95.

Quali cellulari sono compatibili?

http://reader.kaywa.com/phones

Motorola E770, RAZR V3x.

Nokia 3230, 3250, 5300, 6136, 6233, 6260, 6270, 6280, 6288, 6600, 6620, 6630, 6670, 6680, 6681, 6682, 7610, E65, N70, N71, N73, N80, N90, N91, N93, N95.

Samsung SGH-Z500.

SonyEricsson K300i, K510i, K700i, K750i, K800i, S710a, V630, V800, W300i, W550i, W710i, W800i, W810i, W850i, Z520a, Z520i, Z610i.

È gratis?

Si, l'applicazione per leggere i codici è gratuita. Ciò nonostante per accedere ai suoi contenuti è necessario potersi collegare ad Internet attraverso il telefonino. Consultate le tariffe presso il vostro operatore. Si consiglia la connessione a tariffa flat o wireless per scaricare dati.

ＱＲとは、何のコードでしょうか。

ＱＲコードとは、クイック・レスポンス・コードの略で、2次元バーコードのことです。その使用には、コードに含まれている内容を読むためのソフトが必要です。ＱＲコードは、これまでのバーコードと比べると、そのデータ許容量ははるかに増え、文書やリンク、インターネットのページなど大量のデータを格納することができます。

このコードは、誰が主に使うのでしょうか。

ＱＲコードは、2004年に日本で開発され、すでに一般化されています。最近では、ヨーロッパやアメリカでも、カメラを内蔵した携帯電話が普及するにつれて、その使用が始まりました。

Kaywa Readerとは何ですか。

携帯電話のカメラを使ってＱＲコードを読み取るためのアプリケーションです。もっとも、すでに多くの携帯電話のメーカーでは、NOKIA　N95などの新しい機種に、ＱＲコードを読み取るアプリケーションを内臓して販売しています。

以下の機種がコードを読み取るのに使えます。

http://reader.kaywa.com/phones

Nokia 3230, 3250, 5300, 6136, 6233, 6260, 6270, 6280, 6288, 6600, 6620, 6630, 6670, 6680, 6681, 6682, 7610, E65, N70, N71, N73, N80, N90, N91, N93, N95.

Samsung SGH-Z500.

SonyEricsson K300i, K510i, K700i, K750i, K800i, S710a, V630, V800, W300i, W550i, W710i, W800i, W810i, W850i, Z520a, Z520i, Z610i.

このアプリケーションの使用は無料でしょうか。

はい。コードを読み取るアプリケーションは無料です。ただし、内容へのアクセスついては、携帯電話でのインターネットの使用が必要です。契約している会社へその料金や条件をお確かめ下さい。月極め料金かWi-Fiを使用するのがお勧めです。

test here

¿Qué son los códigos QR?

Los códigos QR (Quick Response Codes) son códigos de barras en 2 dimensiones. Es necesario un lector especial para leer su contenido. En comparación con los códigos tradicionales, los QR pueden almacenar mucha información en forma de texto o enlaces a páginas en internet.

¿Quién los utiliza?

Comenzando en 2004, Japón es el país que más utiliza estos códigos de forma masiva. Recientemente, con las nuevas cámaras de los teléfonos móviles se está extendiendo su uso en Europa y América.

¿Qué es el Kaywa Reader?

El Kaywa Reader es una aplicación para móviles que permite leer los códigos QR utilizando la cámara del teléfono móvil. En algunos casos, los fabricantes de teléfonos ya incorporan alguna aplicación para leer estos códigos, como es el caso del Nokia N95.

¿Qué teléfonos son compatibles?

http://reader.kaywa.com/phones

Motorola E770, RAZR V3x.

Nokia 3230, 3250, 5300, 6136, 6233, 6260, 6270, 6280, 6288, 6600, 6620, 6630, 6670, 6680, 6681, 6682, 7610, E65, N70, N71, N73, N80, N90, N91, N93, N95.

Samsung SGH-Z500.

SonyEricsson K300i, K510i, K700i, K750i, K800i, S710a, V630, V800, W300i, W550i, W710i, W800i, W810i, W850i, Z520a, Z520i, Z610i.

¿Es gratis?

Sí, la aplicación para leer los códigos es gratuita. Sin embargo, para acceder a los contenidos es necesario el uso de internet en el móvil. Por favor, consulte las tarifas con su operadora. Es recomendable tener una tarifa plana de datos o utilizar una conexión Wi-Fi.

What are QR codes?

QR (Quick Response codes) codes are barcodes in 2 dimensions. A special reader is necessary for reading its contents. When compared to traditional codes, the QR is capable of storing much information in text format, links and even web pages.

Who uses them?

Starting in 2004, Japan is the country where these codes are most used in a massive way. Thanks to the modern cameras in mobile phones, the QR codes are being widely used in Europe and America.

What is the Kaywa Reader?

The Kaywa Reader is an application in mobiles which allows to reading QR codes by using the mobile phone camera. In some cases, phone manufacturers include some type of application to read these codes, as is the case of Nokia N95.

Which phones are compatible?

http://reader.kaywa.com/phones

Motorola E770, RAZR V3x.

Nokia 3230, 3250, 5300, 6136, 6233, 6260, 6270, 6280, 6288, 6600, 6620, 6630, 6670, 6680, 6681, 6682, 7610, E65, N70, N71, N73, N80, N90, N91, N93, N95.

Samsung SGH-Z500.

SonyEricsson K300i, K510i, K700i, K750i, K800i, S710a, V630, V800, W300i, W550i, W710i, W800i, W810i, W850i, Z520a, Z520i, Z610i.

Is it free of charge?

Yes, the application used to read these codes is free of charge. However, the use of the Internet on the mobile phone is required in order to be able to access to contents. Please, consult your operator for prices. It is advisable to have a data flat rate for data or use a Wi-Fi connection.

Was sind QR-Codes?

QR-Codes (Quick Response Codes) sind zweidimensionale Barcodes. Um ihren Inhalt lesen zu können benötigt man einen speziellen Leser. QR-Codes können im Vergleich zu den herkömmlichen Codes wesentlich mehr Information in Textform oder Links zu Internetseiten speichern.

Wer verwendet sie?

Seit ihrer Einführung 2004 werden diese Codes hauptsächlich in Japan massenweise verwendet. In der letzten Zeit hat sich ihre Verwendung im Zuge der Verbreitung der neuen Mobiltelefonkameras auch in Europa und Amerika ausgeweitet.

Was ist der Kaywa Reader?

Der Kaywa Reader ist eine Anwendung für Mobiltelefone, die das Lesen der QR-Codes mittels der Kamera eines Mobiltelefons erlaubt. In einigen Fällen haben die Hersteller bereits eine Anwendung zum Lesen dieser Codes in die Mobiltelefone integriert, so zum Beispiel bei dem Modell Nokia N95.

Welche Telefone sind kompatibel?

http://reader.kaywa.com/phones

Motorola E770, RAZR V3x.

Nokia 3230, 3250, 5300, 6136, 6233, 6260, 6270, 6280, 6288, 6600, 6620, 6630, 6670, 6680, 6681, 6682, 7610, E65, N70, N71, N73, N80, N90, N91, N93, N95.

Samsung SGH-Z500.

SonyEricsson K300i, K510i, K700i, K750i, K800i, S710a, V630, V800, W300i, W550i, W710i, W800i, W810i, W850i, Z520a, Z520i, Z610i.

Ist diese Anwendung kostenlos?

Ja, die Anwendung zum Lesen der Codes ist kostenlos. Allerdings muss sich das Mobiltelefon ins Internet einwählen, um auf die Inhalte zugreifen zu können. Bitte erkundigen Sie sich bei Ihrem Mobilfunkanbieter über die Preise. Es empfiehlt sich, eine Datenflatrate oder eine drahtlose Netzverbindung (wireless) zu nutzen.

test here

ACERCA DE...

ABOUT...

ÜBER...

À PROPOS DE...

A PROPOSITO DI...

...に関して

Content

HUMAN VISIONS SERIES

War Scenarios

ALL RIGHTS RESERVED 2008, for the first edition in Spanish, English, French, German, Italian and Japanese of

© Netbiblo, S. L.
C/. Rafael Alberti, 6 bajo izq.
Sta. Cristina 15172 Oleiros (La Coruña) – Spain
Tlf: +34 981 91 55 00 • Fax: +34 981 91 55 11
info@bidimobile.com

Bidibooks is a registered trademark of Netbiblo, S. L.

ISBN: 978-84-9745-330-1
Legal Deposit: BI-2014-08

Project Manager: Alexandre Veira Rodríguez
Production Management: Gesbiblo, S. L.
Media Project Management: Bidimobile S. L.
Cover Photo: US Armed Forces

Printed in Spain

ESCENARIOS DE GUERRA

WAR SCENARIOS

KRIEGSSCHAUPLÄTZE

SCÉNARIOS DE GUERRE

SCENARI DI GUERRA

戦争の現場

HUMAN VISIONS SERIES

bidibooks